CRYSTAL PEAKS

Shannon Harvey is the award-winning director of two internationally acclaimed documentaries, *The Connection: Mind Your Body* and *My Year of Living Mindfully*. Her first book, *The Whole Health Life*, explores finding good health after being diagnosed with an autoimmune disease. A journalist and filmmaker, she spent many years working for leading news organisations such as the ABC and Fairfax. Shannon is the recipient of the National Press Club of Australia's 'Health Journalist of the Year' award and now produces a popular blog and podcast, whilst balancing her health and being the mother of two adventurous boys.

MY YEAR OF LIVING MINDFULLY

MY YEAR OF LIVING MINDFULLY

A self-experiment becomes a life-changing experience

SHANNON HARVEY

hachette
AUSTRALIA

Published in Australia and New Zealand in 2020
by Hachette Australia
(an imprint of Hachette Australia Pty Limited)
Level 17, 207 Kent Street, Sydney NSW 2000
www.hachette.com.au

10 9 8 7 6 5 4 3 2 1

Copyright © Shannon Harvey 2020

A catalogue record for this
book is available from the
National Library of Australia

ISBN: 978 0 7336 4509 9 (paperback)

Cover design by Christabella Designs and Elemental Media
Cover photograph courtesy Julian Harvey/Elemental Media
Typeset in Garamond Regular by Kirby Jones

Printed and bound in Great Britain by Clays Ltd, Elcograf S.p.A.

The paper this book is printed on is certified against the Forest Stewardship Council® Standards. McPherson's Printing Group holds FSC® chain of custody certification SA-COC-005379. FSC® promotes environmentally responsible, socially beneficial and economically viable management of the world's forests.

For my teachers …

Justine Latham – My high school geography teacher who gave me curiosity and wonder about the world's places and people. Thank you for bending the rules so that I could hand in a documentary instead of an essay for my final assignment. You were the spark.

Peter Manning – My journalism professor who showed me how to channel my youthful longing to solve problems into something coherent and useful. You taught me about the importance of truth and balance, and the how of great storytelling.

Patrick Kearney – My mindfulness meditation teacher who, with surgical precision, taught me how to hear myself think. Your patience, wisdom and insight changed everything.

And for my kids, Theo and Izzy …

I intend to put what I've been taught to good use and do what I can to make the world you will inherit a little better.

CONTENTS

INTRODUCTION

Now and Zen

As the true method of knowledge is experiment, the true faculty of knowing must be the faculty which experiences.

— William Blake, All Religions Are One,
'The Argument' (1788)[1]

The first draft of this book began in very much the same way as the documentary film I made with the same title. It explained that the spark for my year of living mindfully originated from an intention to tackle a big problem: the global mental health crisis.

Despite living in a time of unprecedented progress in science, technology and medicine, at the time my project began, the leading medical science journal *The Lancet* had just published a special issue declaring that every country in the world was facing and failing to tackle a host of mental health issues.[2] As I write these words three years later, we are still falling short. More people die by suicide than are killed by soldiers, terrorists or criminals combined, and unless we change course, by 2030 depression is on track to overtake heart disease as our single biggest health problem.[3,4]

It's true that these troubling facts on their own would be a worthy motivator for any unshrinking health journalist embarking on a new investigative deep dive, but as I read over the first iteration of this book, I knew I wasn't telling the whole story – because behind the mental health facts and statistics lies a personal and painful lived experience that influences everything I do.

Throughout my childhood I witnessed the devastating effects of severe depression, addiction, and bipolar disorder firsthand. I visited some of the people I loved most in the world in psych wards and rehab clinics, and I attended the funerals of family members who, unable to bear the burden of their suffering, had taken their own lives. I experienced unforgettable trauma that took me years to process. For me, like so many others, the wounds of mental illness run deep.

At age 24, during an especially lonely period in my life when I was living far away from family and friends, I was diagnosed with an autoimmune disease, which was originally thought to be lupus (SLE). Over the years different doctors have given my illness different labels, such as fibromyalgia, connective tissue disorder, or more recently Sjögren's syndrome, but whatever the label, my incurable autoimmune illness means that I'm facing a lifetime of chronic pain caused by arthritic inflammation throughout my body.

The truth is I wanted to investigate real-life solutions and find trustworthy information to help others, but I also wanted to find answers for myself. And it wasn't just my future I was thinking about. I wanted to be able to teach my kids how to prepare themselves for the world they'll go out into. With a family history of mental illness and addiction, and as they face a future of increasing uncertainty, how could they nurture, nourish and protect their minds?

Although there was tonnes of information on what we should all be eating and drinking, how much sleep we should be getting and how much exercise we should be doing to maintain our physical wellbeing, when I looked for a widely accepted, evidence-based recommendation for our mental health – the brain's equivalent of a 30-minute jog around the block, or the mind's daily serving of five fruit and vegetables – I found *nothing*.

While the role of things such as diet, sleep, exercise and social support are recommended for good mental health, I needed something more concrete; a kind of psychological fitness training.

Like so many people, my To Do list was insane. After having my second baby, between all the mothering and wife-ing, cleaning and cooking, friending, sistering, daughtering, event attending and exercising – let alone the full-time working – life was getting the better of me. It wasn't so much that I had a severe mental illness – I wasn't in the grip of a major depressive episode, a drug addiction, or post-traumatic stress flashbacks; day to day, I was functioning – it's just that I wasn't *flourishing*. On a wellbeing scale developed by American sociologist and psychologist from Emory University Professor Corey Keyes, which measures mental health as a continuum, I put myself as feeling below halfway.[5]

What finally motivated me to make a change was the chronic pain from my illness, which was threatening to flare up, and my insomnia. One or two nights a week my mind would get caught up, repetitively going over my worries without end, and I was unable to sleep.

3

THE MENTAL HEALTH CONTINUUM

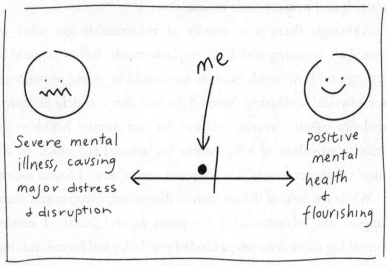

me

Severe mental illness, causing major distress & disruption ⟵——•——⟶ positive mental health & flourishing

#Keyes CLM. The mental health continuum: from languishing to flourishing in life. J Health Soc Behav. 2002, 43 (2): 207-222.

Looking back, I really should have known better. I'm a *health* journalist, after all. I've made a film called *The Connection* and written a book called *The Whole Health Life*, both of which showed that when it comes to good health, our mind and body are inextricably connected. And yet, I wasn't doing a very good job at taking care of my own psychological needs, let alone anyone else's. As every flight attendant will tell you, when the plane's going down put on your own oxygen mask first before trying to help others. It was time to get back on track.

I knew I was ticking the boxes on the healthy living guidelines. Whole-food, plant-rich diet. Tick. Regular exercise. Tick. Strong relationships and supportive husband. Tick. Regularly spending time in nature. Tick. Meaningful work. Tick. What was missing?

With both professional and personal motivational forces driving me on, I began my search. I first considered finding a good therapist. But although one-on-one TLC had once helped me process and understand my troubled past, and may have again helped me to find clarity around the looping worries now keeping me awake at night, it wasn't going to do anything for my arthritic pain or help me protect the mental wellbeing of my kids. I imagined the call ...

Hello, my name is Shannon and I'd like to book my children in for some psychology lessons please. What's that? Are they experiencing any symptoms of mental distress at the moment? Well, no ... Have they experienced trauma? Fortunately, no. Have they been diagnosed with depression or anxiety? No, they're fine at the moment. But based on the statistics and our family history, they are very likely to suffer at some point in their lives and I'm hoping I can do something about it beforehand. Aren't there some kind of mental resilience exercises you can give them?

Even if there were such a thing as 'preventative psychology', when I did some basic mathematics based on global data I realised that if all the available qualified psychiatrists and psychologists worked 24/7, they'd only be able to spend one hour with each of us once every five years. For the big-picture mental health issues I was trying to work out, individual therapy – both prevention and treatment – was unrealistic for an already overburdened medical system.

It was clear that any workable solution would need to meet some key requirements. It had to:

- Be free or at least affordable.
- Be available to anyone, regardless of their education or life circumstances.
- Realistically and flexibly fit into people's busy schedules.
- Be based on scientific evidence.

That was a lot to ask for in my search for the equivalent of a healthy eating plan for my mind, but of them all, the most important was that it would be grounded in science.

I was diagnosed with my illness in 2004. Essentially, my rogue immune system attacks my own body's healthy tissue, causing arthritis throughout my body. When I first fell ill, I walked with a limp because I felt so sore. Other days I couldn't get out of bed.

It wasn't until I was in my late 20s, after I'd been sick for a number of years and had spent tens of thousands of dollars on alternative therapies, that I finally started to learn about the importance of scientific thinking. After one particularly unscrupulous company used pseudoscience to sell me a fake cure, I realised that I needed to apply to my own health the same critical thinking skills that I'd been using every day working as a journalist.[6]

I began to read academic papers in peer-reviewed journals, to go to the source of the science, and to never trust an 'expert' who was unwilling to elaborate enthusiastically on what their cure *couldn't* do. I also learned that when it comes to health, a treatment becomes 'evidence based' when it is backed up by objective data that proves it is effective.

Slowly but surely, over a number of years, I made science-backed lifestyle changes to areas in my life such as my diet, exercise habits, sleep routines and work hours. It's now been 14 years since I was told I had an incurable illness and although I do experience painful flares on occasion, especially when things in my life get hectic or I'm overly stressed and emotional, I don't need medication for my illness and my days spent bed-ridden are a thing of the past.

I have science and the evidence-based guidance it has provided me to thank for that. It's been my trusted guide through the murky waters of the wellness industry.

So, with my non-negotiable requisites that the mental health solution I was looking for had to be affordable, widely available, realistic, flexible, *and* science-backed, it seemed at first my search would be futile. But it turned out there was one thing that might just fulfil my wish list – mindfulness meditation.

We have decades of research backing up advice on exercise, sleep and nutrition, but meditation research has only really kicked off in the last 10 years. In that time, the body of evidence has exploded from a few hundred peer-reviewed papers to over six thousand.[7]

And this is what I found *really* interesting: consistent, empirical evidence demonstrated that an eight-week program, underpinned by mindfulness training, can be equal to drugs for preventing recurrent depression. There were also promising

THE GROWING RISE OF MINDFULNESS RESEARCH

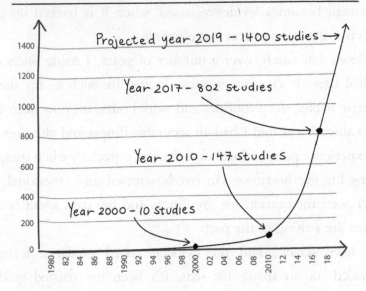

Projected year 2019 – 1400 studies →

Year 2017 – 802 studies

Year 2010 – 147 studies

Year 2000 – 10 studies

*according to the The PubMed online database (pubmed.gov)

results in experiments using mindfulness in the treatment of chronic pain[8], stress[9], anxiety[10] and addiction.[11]

Given our mental health crisis, I wondered if regular mental training, such as mindfulness, could be a missing link. Should we all be practising mindfulness in the same way that we exercise and eat our vegetables? Or is the evidence too good to be true? What would happen if I committed to mindfulness in the same way I've committed to physical activity and a healthy diet? What would happen to my health and wellbeing if I meditated every day for a year?

After several weeks of thinking, talking and seeking advice from medical and mental health professionals, as well as academics and researchers alike, it became clear that there was only one way to find out once and for all. I set up a rigorous, complicated, absurdly expensive and hare-brained, world-first experiment, which became known as:

My Year of Living Mindfully.

CHAPTER ONE

No Time Like the Present

Experiment Background

When I was shooting *The Connection* in 2013, I interviewed two scientists independently acknowledged for bringing mainstream credibility to meditation in the West. Each encounter left me with a growing certainty that mind–body skills, such as meditation, could play an important role in medicine of the future.[1]

First, I met renegade MD and Harvard scholar Herbert Benson, who in the late 1960s snuck Transcendental meditators through the back door of his lab and discovered that his human guinea pigs were eliciting a relaxation response, opposite to the fight-or-flight stress response. Shortly after, I met microbiologist turned mindfulness meditation teacher Jon Kabat-Zinn, who in the 1970s developed an eight-week program called Mindfulness Based Stress Reduction (MBSR) in order to help people with chronic illnesses who were falling through the cracks of a reductionist healthcare system.

More recently, researchers at the Benson-Henry Institute for Mind Body Medicine at Massachusetts General Hospital published a promising study showing that practising the relaxation response technique could 'downregulate' (turn down the volume control on) genes associated with chronic inflammation. The MBSR program has now been shown to improve everything from anxiety and depression, to quality of life and burnout.[2] Consequently, MBSR is embedded into the fabric of many hospitals, schools and even parliaments.

Although they told me that their findings were just a starting point and that more research was needed, meeting these two men, who had been instrumental in what *Time* magazine was hailing as the 'Mindful Revolution', was enough to convince me to give meditation a go.[3] My logic was that I could hopefully counteract the harmful effects of all the stress in my life by setting aside 10 or 20 minutes each day to intentionally relax.

In the years since, despite my good intentions, my problem has always been *sticking* with the practice. As I write these words, in the 14 months since the birth of my second son, Isaac (Izzy), I haven't even attempted to find the time to meditate. I confess that I've probably partly invented this whole year-of-living-mindfully experiment in order to determine once and for all if finding the time to meditate is actually *worth* it. With my To Do list already full, can daily meditation really make a difference?

The last few months have been a whirlwind of phone calls, emails and late-night Skype calls with researchers all around the world. I'm finally ready to put my hypothesis to the test. If I'm going to dedicate myself to this project for what will be close to the next 18 months, then I'm going to do it right.

I have set up interviews with 18 of the world's top mindfulness scientists to guide me and also convinced an additional six Australian researchers, as well as my doctor, to track all the key bio-markers that have been linked to mindfulness. If the evidence is anything to go by, regular mindfulness meditation should, theoretically, have positive effects on my mind, body and health.

THE TEAM

Mentor

CRAIG HASSED, MBBS, FRACGP, OAM
Associate Professor, Monash University
Mindfulness Coordinator, Department of General Practice

Craig has been instrumental in introducing a variety
of innovations into medical education and practice in
Australia and overseas, and was the founding president of
the Australian Teachers of Meditation Association. He's
written no less than 13 books related to lifestyle medicine.
Craig and I met in 2012 after I came across a document he
had written that changed my life. At the time I was very
sick and had spent a fortune trying everything that both
conventional and alternative medicine had to offer. On
about page 20 of a Google search I found a paper which
was called 'Mind-Body Medicine: Science, Practice and
Philosophy' that Craig had written for medical students
enrolled in his course at Monash University.[4] It outlined

---

research linking the brain to the immune system, the importance of group support in improving outcomes for sick people, and how stress reduction techniques (such as meditation) could improve immune function. It gave me a credible, reliable, and trustworthy path to follow. Over the years he's become a friend and mentor, and for this experiment he's generously spent hours on the phone with me from Melbourne, advising what tests would be meaningful and the ideal kinds of scientists to try to recruit.

Scientists

NICOLAS CHERBUIN, PhD

Professor, Centre of Research Excellence in Cognitive Health, Australian National University

Head, Centre for Research on Ageing, Health and Wellbeing

Nic will be using magnetic resonance imaging (MRI) and functional magnetic resonance imaging (fMRI) to track my brain structure and function.

NEIL BAILEY, PhD

Adjunct Research Fellow, Alfred Psychiatry Research Centre Monash University

Neil will be using electroencephalogram (EEG) to track my attention and working memory.

MARC WILKINS, PhD

Professor, School of Biotechnology and Biomolecular Sciences, University of New South Wales

Director, Ramaciotti Centre for Genomics

Marc will be examining the expression of 17 000 genes in my white blood cells. Marc coined the term 'proteome' in 1994, while developing the concept as a PhD student, so he must be very clever.

HILDA PICKETT, PhD
Associate Professor, University of Sydney
Head of the Telomere Length Regulation Unit,
Children's Medical Research Institute

In the name of rigorous science, Hilda will be using no less than *three* different techniques to study my cellular ageing by measuring my telomeres, which are the little protective caps that sit on the end of my DNA. The shorter my telomeres, the more chance there is for having a chronic illness.

MARC LONGSTER, PhD
Stratech Scientific APAC

Marc will be running hundreds of tests, tracking my salivary stress hormones and immune function, as well as the cortisol in my hair samples. He's the reason I'll soon have bald patches all over my head. Great.

KIMINA LYALL
Doctor of Psychology (clinical) candidate
Deakin University

Kimina is interested in how mindfulness might impact my subjective wellbeing and quality of life. She thinks mindfulness might be restorative when we're knocked off our normal wellbeing baseline.

ANNA FINNISS, MD
Rheumatologist

Anna is my specialist autoimmune disease doctor. Although she wonders how I'm going to find the time to meditate in my already very busy life, she'll be keeping an eye on my illness markers and symptoms.

Guinea pig

SHANNON HARVEY
Journalist, filmmaker, insomniac

Starting with a series of baseline tests, over the next 12 months I'll be poked, prodded, scanned and screened more than 100 times. The team will track my stress hormones, immune system, gene expression, cellular ageing and subjective wellbeing. Perhaps the most interesting test of all, though, will be seeing what happens to my brain.

From a neuroscientific viewpoint, meditation is a systematic form of mental training. Theoretically, when I repeatedly do something, there's activity in my brain, which over time changes my brain structure. It's the old 'neurons that fire together, wire together' catchphrase and it doesn't matter if I'm practising the piano[5], learning to navigate London streets in a taxi cab[6], or meditating: the research on neuroplasticity shows that if I practise something over and over, my brain should change.

Several studies have used magnetic resonance imaging (MRI) to compare the brain structure of long-term meditators with novices, and there are fascinating differences. Professor Nicolas Cherbuin, an expert in brain ageing from the Australian National University in Canberra and one of the two neuroscientists studying my brain over the next year, was involved in one study which found that at age 50 the brains of meditators were seven and a half years younger than those of non-meditators.[7]

When I first read this study I thought, *Younger brain? Woo hoo. I'm* in. But it's not so simple. Nic and his colleagues noted that their findings only led to more questions. Perhaps the brains of the meditators were different because they also did more physical exercise or had varying degrees of education? Maybe they were more inclined to stick with meditation because they had unique brains to begin with?

The missing link here, in not only the neuroscientific research on mindfulness but also the psychological and biological research, is studies that track meditation beginners, like me, over time.

Experiment Methodology

I'm starting with 20 minutes of mindfulness training a day and will slowly build from there. I'll experiment with a variety of apps until I find one that suits me. I've signed up for an eight-week MBSR course and a 10-day silent retreat. Apart from that, nothing else will change. I'll still have my usual parenting duties and work commitments, which include travelling, interviewing, and writing full time, and I won't alter my diet or exercise habits.

As for the actual practice – I'm turning to the experts.

MEDITATION JOURNAL, DAY 3

Time: *20 minutes daily*
Method: *Ten Percent Happier meditation app*
Technique: *Guided breath awareness meditation with teacher Sharon Salzberg*

Experiment notes:
Sharon is teaching me the basics by having me focus on my breath. I get distracted. Whoops. This is actually quite hard. Back to the breath. Thoughts about the interview I need to prep. Thoughts about the blog I need to write. Thoughts about how bad I am at this. Thoughts about thoughts. Thoughts about

---

the fact that the breath isn't relaxing. Thoughts about wanting this to end. When will it be over? Plane noise overhead ... Argh! Realise I'm distracted. But wait, Sharon just said that's the point – the remembering to come back to focus. Okay. All good. Back to the breath. I can do this. Wait, I'm distracted again. Diiiing. Time's up! Wow, that was awful. It's going to be a long year ...

What Is Mindfulness, Anyway?

Some people have told me that mindfulness is a life-saving psychological tool that pulled them out of the depths of depression. Others have said it's a way of disentangling from the grip of addiction. Some use mindfulness to face chronic pain or stressful emotions, while others use it to achieve peak performance at work. I've heard mindfulness described as an innate human capability of such great importance that it should be taught in schools, while others see it merely as a marketing device used to sell colouring books.

I'm finding the kaleidoscopic array of definitions baffling. Given that I'm interested in mindfulness because of the emerging evidence in support of its life-changing benefits for mental and physical health, it's surprising that I can't find a unified scientific definition, nor any broad agreement on its underlying concepts. Defining mindfulness, it seems, is a bit like defining complex ideas such as 'intelligence'[8] and 'wisdom'[9] – very little is universally accepted.

In my search for clarity, I got back in touch with mindfulness pioneer Jon Kabat-Zinn, because his definition is probably the most widely used and accepted by scientists and mindfulness teachers alike. 'My working definition of mindfulness – this is what I call an "operational" definition – is the awareness that arises from paying attention on purpose, in the present moment, non-judgementally,' he says. 'It's an operational definition because when you put it into operation, then mindfulness arises within you.'

Jon's operational definition clarifies why, in psychological science at least, mindfulness can be regarded as a state of mind, a personality trait, a meditation practice, and a mental health intervention.[10] He intentionally allows for complexity so that it can be picked apart and studied in differing combinations such as acceptance, attentiveness, awareness, focus, curiosity, or attitude.

But there's a big difference between understanding mindfulness in theory and putting it into practice. I've read umpteen books and listened to countless talks about 'the power of now', but in my efforts to 'be in the moment', I can't work out exactly what moment I'm supposed to be in. At any given time there's an infinite choice of things that I can pay attention to: sounds, smells, sensations, even my thoughts and feelings all happen 'in the moment'.

Even if I manage to pick one thing – the feeling of my breath on my nostrils, for example – remaining focused is proving impossible. Sometime later – maybe five minutes, maybe 10 – I wake up from any number of runaway thought trains, from the practical (*How long should I soak the cashews in order to make that sauce*

tomorrow?), to the worthy (*The conclusions of that stress-immune health review paper could be really interesting for my readers with chronic illnesses*), to the trivially inconsequential (*Does Meghan Markle get a wardrobe allowance from the UK government?*).

Even more befuddling is the scientific literature which reveals that being 'in the moment' is probably impossible thanks to the hardwired ways our brains process thinking and decision-making.[11] Because of something called the 'flash lag effect', my consciousness lingers around 80 milliseconds behind actual events. Put simply, by the time I'm consciously aware of it, the present is already in the past.[12] I asked my mentor Craig about this problem and he sagely advised me not to get too caught up, because science currently struggles to measure consciousness. He explained that the 'present moment' will always be gone before my mind knows it is there. My conclusion? The 'moment' is a misnomer.

So where to turn next? The most useful metaphor I've found comes from Daniel Siegel, clinical professor of psychiatry at the UCLA School of Medicine and a leading mindfulness advocate. Siegel has us think of our awareness as lying at the centre of a circle (the 'hub') from which, at any given time, we can focus on any number of thoughts, feelings, and sensations circling us on the 'rim'.[13]

Everything that we could be aware of is represented on the outer rim and the experience of being aware is represented in the hub. Mindfulness training is about intentionally connecting the hub and rim via a 'spoke' of attention, which can be directed to focus on one point or another on the rim.

DANIEL SIEGEL'S
WHEEL OF AWARENESS

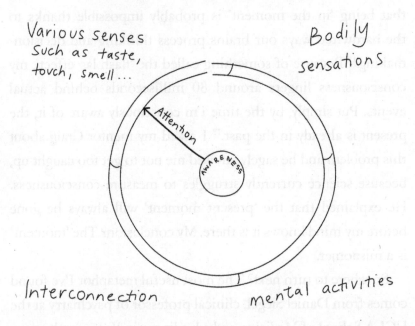

Various senses
such as taste,
touch, smell...

Bodily
sensations

Attention

AWARENESS

Interconnection

mental activities

*Villamil A, Vogel T, Weisbaum E, Siegel D. Cultivating Well-Being through the Three Pillars of Mind Training: Understanding How Training the Mind Improves Physiological and Psychological Well-being. OBM Integrative and Complementary Medicine. 2019;4:1-1.

Framed in this way, mindfulness training involves intentionally calling on my awareness instead of being lost in thought out on the rim. I'm starting to understand why a variety of meditation techniques can be used, whether it's a body scan ('... *bring your attention to your left toe* ...'), breath awareness ('... *notice the feeling of air on your nostrils* ...'), open awareness ('... *what is passing through your experience moment to moment?* ...') or an infinite number of other non-judgemental awareness techniques. The point is to practise *intentionally* directing my attention and to become more connected with my awareness.

Others have articulated this better than me. Journalist turned meditation app entrepreneur Dan Harris told me that practising mindfulness is like sitting behind a flowing waterfall, aware of the gushing waters that are our thoughts and experiences.

.I also like author/self-experimentalist Tim Ferriss's analogy that being mindful is like sitting outside of a washing machine. When he's caught up in his thoughts he's in the washing machine, but by being mindful he's able to step outside and become aware of his tumbling experiences as they occur.[14]

All this came together for me today when I sat down to practice and listened to the words of Amercian mindfulness teacher Sharon Salzberg, speaking to me in my headphones when I loaded my meditation app:

> If something arises that is strong enough to take your
> attention away from the feeling of the breath, you fall asleep,
> or you get lost in some incredible fantasy – the moment you
> realise you've been distracted is the magic moment because
> that's the moment you have the chance to be really different.
> Not judge yourself, not put yourself down. But simply let
> go and begin again. If you have to let go and begin again

thousands of times, that's fine. That's the practice. That's the training.

— Sharon Salzberg, 'Being Mindful of Distractions' meditation, Ten Percent Happier app

A Goal Without A Plan Is Just A Wish

Surprisingly, the biggest problem with this mindful experiment is not convincing a bunch of experts to donate their time and study me for a year, nor even coming up with the $30000 to cover the costs of their lab time and tests. My biggest problem is that I have *no* idea how I'm going to find the time to meditate.

I'm not the only one with this problem. I've been looking into the stats on the likelihood of my success and it turns out that making a lifestyle change like this is really, *really* hard. Depending on what it is I'm trying to change, there's a 50 to 80 per cent chance I will fail, most likely within the first month.[15,16]

I'm hoping that I'll be able to 'science my way' into finding magic minutes in my day, but despite all the 'Five Science-Backed Ways To ... Blah Blah Blah' catchy clickbait headlines on social media, it turns out experts know very little about the keys to sustained behaviour change. One review, which took into account the top 100 behaviour theories being used in respected academic circles, concluded that, 'It is currently unclear what conditions are required to maintain the new behaviour and prevent relapse, or to re-establish the new behaviour after relapse.'[17] Great. Thanks, science.

There is, however, some research that *hints* at a way forward. When I was writing *The Whole Health Life*, I interviewed behaviour change expert Peter Gollwitzer, a professor of psychology at New York University. Peter has developed a technique called 'If-Then' planning to help us bridge the gap between what we *intend* to do and what we *actually* do. The idea is simple and involves three steps. Essentially, I have to specify:

- the action I intend to take,
- when and where I will undertake it, and
- what I'll do when I slip up.

I suspect that over time my If-Then planning will evolve, but for now, it looks like this:

If it's 6.00 a.m. when I wake, *then* I will get up and meditate in my living room for 20 minutes.

If I need to sleep in a bit longer or the kids wake up early, *then* I will meditate at work on my lunch break.

If it's the weekend and I'm not at work, *then* I will meditate in my home office while my one-year-old son has his nap and my four-year-old son is listening to an audiobook.

If my day has been too busy and I still haven't meditated, *then* I will meditate in my bedroom as soon as the kids are in bed.

I'm guessing that three out of seven days a week I'll manage to meditate first thing in the morning, two days I'll meditate on my lunch break at work, and two days I'll go all the way through to the end of the day before finding the time.

I also suspect that if I planned to meditate at the exact same time each and every day, I would fail. I don't have a regular and scheduled life, so by having this backup If-Then strategy, I should theoretically be able to establish a daily practice.

There is a big hitch to all this, though. While Peter's review of 94 studies on the effectiveness of the If-Then strategy showed promising results, it's too simplistic to conclude that a little bit of planning is all I need to do in order to establish a yearlong meditation habit. Indeed, many of the studies were combined with studies of other motivational strategies, including boosting self-belief and having positive experiences.[18,19]

It's this *positive experiences* bit that especially bothers me. Pretty much anyone who has tried to continually focus their distracted mind will agree that it's more like wrestling with the proverbial monkey than being all 'glowing balls of light' or 'a warm bath for your mind', as it's sometimes described. In a world flooded with Pinterest boards and heroic Highlanders on Netflix, it's going to be very difficult to *choose* to meditate after a long day at work when the kids are finally in bed.

This is where I hope the support of my husband, Jules, will help. If my willpower wanes, hopefully his gentle encouragement will steer me back on track. Failing that, I'll keep in mind the advice given to me by Associate Professor Amishi Jah from the University of Miami, who's a full-time working mother, like I am, and a leading mindfulness neuroscientist. 'It's like flossing,' she told me. 'If you can commit to flossing one tooth, your dental health will improve. Why? Because nobody flosses one tooth. You're there, you're ready to go, you're going to do the full routine. I think that if you keep your bar very low, of just sitting on the cushion once a day, just taking the posture of practising [meditation], even if you get up after that, with that as your requirement for your day, I think that you're likely to have a lot of success with this in the next year.'

FOUR WAYS I'M GOING TO SET A HEALTH GOAL

(And Actually Stick With It)

1. Commit

My favourite anecdote about making lasting healthy changes comes from a fellow self-experimentalist/author, A.J. Jacobs, who wanted to overcome his addiction to dried mango slices. He'd tried several strategies to kick the habit but nothing worked. In the end he wrote a $1000 cheque to the American Nazi Party and made his wife promise to mail it if he ate another dried mango. This is called a 'commitment contract', a concept in which the 'me' of today doesn't trust the 'me' of tomorrow.[20] Throughout my year of living mindfully I've enlisted the help of a team of scientists who are tracking my every move. If I fail there won't be anything interesting for the scientists to find, and I may as well flush the $30000 investment in lab time down the toilet. It's elaborate, I know, but A.J. recently emailed me from New York to say that he's never touched a dried mango slice since he made his commitment contract with the American Nazi Party, so I think he might be onto something.

2. Plan

Professor Peter Gollwitzer from New York University will help me overcome the gap between what I intend to do and what I will actually do.

*If*_____, *then* _____.

And *if*_____ fails, *then* _____.

3. Sacrifice

There aren't enough hours in a day to do everything on my 'Should Do' list, so something will have to give. At times I'll probably be relinquishing sleep, or my lunch break, but more often than not I suspect that I'll be meditating instead of being buried in social media or watching television.

4. Recruit on three levels

Practical – I've enlisted Jules, who's said he's willing to be left with a sink full of dirty dishes when necessary so that I can meditate before I turn into a pumpkin. Among other things, he's also going to keep the home fires burning when I join an eight-week meditation course for a few hours on Sunday afternoons and when I go away on a silent retreat later in the year.

Emotional – I'm concerned that becoming 'a meditator' might be lonely because I might sound like a fruitcake, or a better-than-you know-it-all when I'm talking about it with others. I'll need the support of people I'm close to including Jules, Teeny (my sister, Justine) and Liz (my best friend). I think they'll be honest enough to tell me if I've gone too far, but encouraging enough to keep me on track.

Informational – In an age of information overload, finding good teachers, books, podcasts and apps will be important. I'll do my research and turn only to trusted sources for recommendations.

With the interviews lined up, the scientific A-Team assembled, and a solid plan for success, what do I rate as my chance of success? 50 per cent.

CHAPTER TWO

Mind the Hype

MEDITATION JOURNAL, DAY 14

Time: *20 minutes daily*

Method: *Ten Percent Happier meditation app*

Technique: *2 x 10-minute breath awareness meditations led by Sharon Salzberg and Joseph Goldstein*

Experiment notes:

Noticing breath at my nostrils. In. Out. In. Out. To Do
list starts. Achievements and shortcomings. Ambitions and
inadequacies. What I have and have not done today. What I will
or will not do tomorrow. Begin again. Breath. Breath. In. Out.
I should be better at this by now, surely. Begin again. Breath.
Breath. In. Out. What did I expect anyway? Superhuman
powers of focus? More productivity in my day? Sunshine and
rainbows? My Too-Much-To-Do-and-Not-Enough-Time-To-
Do-It list hasn't magically evaporated. Argh. Begin again.
Diiiing. And time is up.

McMindfulness

Starting with the good news, Peter Gollwitzer's If–Then planning technique (and a small army of scientists holding me to account) has meant that I haven't *yet* missed a day. But honestly, I'm really not *enjoying* meditation and I don't think I'm getting any better at it.

I am, however, learning that mindfulness is essentially a 3500-year-old technique to teach me how my mind works. But now that I'm looking into it, there's just so much mindfulness on offer and it's hard to know where to start and who to trust.

Meditation is now the fastest growing[1] health trend in the US and has transformed from an ancient spiritual practice into a 1.2-billion-dollar industry.[2] Unlike other meditation techniques, such as Transcendental Meditation, mindfulness has never been trademarked and it's therefore now widely available everywhere from classrooms to boardrooms, in studios and online. There are mindful books, apps, podcasts, gyms, busses and even mayonnaise. In my search for trustworthy information and hard facts, this is a big red flag.

At one end of the spectrum there are eight-week mindfulness courses being delivered in healthcare settings by certified teachers. At the other end is a pot-pie-based meditation system that promises to 'nourish my mind and body' that was released on YouTube by a cheeky team of jesting advertisers in the marketing department at KFC.[3]

I've found books on mindful parenting, beauty, drinking, lawyering, politics, marketing, money management, insurance, dog ownership, toilet training and divorce secrets, which is not to say they aren't informative, but I suspect that if the first person to teach mindfulness (a man named Siddhārtha Gautama, aka 'The Buddha') were around today, he probably wouldn't recognise the systematic training method for relieving suffering that he originally came up with under a fig tree in north-eastern India all those centuries ago.

With more than 100 000 products now capitalising on the word 'mindfulness' for sale on Amazon (including the *Mindful Pets Tear Stain Remover Combs for Dogs* and the *Mindfull Products Space Saving Wine Bottle Rack*), I'm not surprised that the mindfulness movement is copping a backlash. I'm drawn to academic articles with intriguing headlines such as 'Is Mindfulness the New Opiate of the Masses? Critical Reflections from a Buddhist Perspective' and I'm fascinated that there's even an emerging *anti*-mindfulness industry complete with conferences, blogs and bestselling books, which all promote scepticism and disbelief.[4]

The self-titled 'Mindful Crank', Ron Purser, a management professor from San Francisco State University, has become a leading voice of the critics and cynics after writing two provocative articles for *Salon* and the *Huffington Post*.[5–7] Purser is also an ordained Zen Dharma teacher and is concerned that superficial 'McMindfulness' dangerously ignores the ethical Buddhist foundations and traditions from which the practice originally emerged.

His main argument is that because secular mindfulness is stripped of potentially unpopular religious notions (such as abstaining from killing and stealing, and avoiding work that harms living creatures) and because teachers are emphasising the 'non-judgement' part of the training, mindfulness has turned into a banal, faux-therapeutic, self-help fad. Purser also thinks that the training is being widely used by unscrupulous corporations for the purposes of making employees more efficient and docile within stressful work environments.

After the social media buzz (aka a highly marketable fuss) and the subsequent launch of his *Mindful Cranks* podcast, I wasn't surprised that his book titled *McMindfulness* became available for sale on Amazon. But despite the paradox that Purser is forging a career out of criticising people for making money off mindfulness, he does raise some good points.

Following this line of thinking, we (myself now included) could theoretically be taught a kind of mental training that is more harmful that helpful. At best, this could mean that we waste our money on self-help drivel. At worst, this could mean that those of us working in tyrannical organisations (who actually need things such as paid vacation leave or flexible working hours) become more compliant instead of taking action. And at very worst, this could mean that we're taught to be desensitised from natural altruistic human emotions, instincts and values, and subsequently turn evil.

With all this stewing in my mind, I found myself backstage at Sydney's annual Happiness and Its Causes Conference in the company of the French-born Buddhist monk Matthieu Ricard. Matthieu, who's usually based in a monastery in the mountains of Nepal, is a former molecular geneticist who now operates a charity with 200 humanitarian projects underway. He's been invited to present at the elite World Economic Forum (WEF), held in a Swiss ski resort in Davos, nine times, so I thought his perspective on McMindfulness would be especially salient.

'Any tool can be used to do good or to do harm,' Matthieu told me. 'A hammer can be used to build a beautiful house, or to put a nail to hang some beautiful things. It can also be used to destroy, or to smash someone's brains. A litre of petrol can be used to travel to a beautiful place, or to set ablaze a house with people inside. Likewise, unfortunately, mind training can be reverse mind training.'

According to Matthieu, the activities of psychopaths, burglars and snipers could all be said to be carried out in a focused, present-minded, non-judgemental way. 'But if you just add six letters – c.a.r.i.n.g. – then you have right mindfulness,' he explained. 'You don't have caring snipers and caring psychopaths. That's why, when you train your mind, the ethical aspect is *so* important. It has to be all for removing suffering and bringing good to sentient beings, otherwise you become a totally merciless killer.'

This *caring* mindfulness is what Matthieu emphasises when he's talking to CEOs and world leaders. 'There's nothing to lose and everything to gain, and you get two for the price of one,' he said before going on stage.

As I listened to the red-robed monk ardently encourage an audience of about 1800 psychologists, health coaches and wellbeing consultants to cultivate mindfulness and compassion for the good of themselves, their families and the planet, I realised that mindfulness is a skill, in the same way that reading is a skill. Just as reading teaches me to understand words on a page, mindfulness teaches me to know how my mind works. What I choose to do with the skills I learn – what books I read, what thoughts I think; for good or bad, better or worse –

will ultimately be influenced by my own moral code and values, as well as those of the teachers I choose.

Mindfulness Is A Meaningless Word With Shoddy Science Behind It ...

Facts do not cease to exist because they are ignored.

– Aldous Huxley, Complete Essays 2 (1926-29)[8]

A few weeks after my encounter with Matthieu I thought that my mindful experiment was getting back on track, but I've now hit a more troubling predicament. Ron Purser's McMindfulness concerns are gaining momentum. Just arrived in my inbox is a scientific paper written by 15 well-respected neuroscientists, mindfulness researchers and meditation teachers called 'Mind the Hype', which has inspired a series of provocative headlines such as 'Mindfulness Is A Meaningless Word With Shoddy Science Behind It' and 'Is Mindfulness Meditation BS?'[9,10]

The paper's main message is that the science of mindfulness is being over-sold and over-hyped because much of the research is underpowered and poorly designed. The paper claims that the 'compelling' stress reduction and wellbeing evidence is limited and that the jury is still out on whether meditation boosts attention and memory. The authors highlight evidence that mindfulness and meditation can sometimes be harmful, and that, as I already discovered in the first month of this experiment, there's no scientific consensus on what mindfulness actually is.

This is even more concerning than I first realised because not having a unified definition dilutes the significance of the evidence. In the same way that organic goji berries from the mountains of Tibet and hydroponic tomatoes grown in space are both called 'fruit', different types of practice can be called 'mindfulness'. In much of the scientific literature they're actually comparing the mindfulness equivalents of apples and oranges.[11]

In my efforts to understand the potential for mindfulness for mental and physical health, this *really* matters. In the four years since I released my last film and book I have talked and written extensively about the scientifically 'validated' health benefits of meditation. But the 'Mind the Hype' paper and the subsequent commentary is forcing me to question everything.[12] I thought I was reporting on reliable solutions, educating people, and making the world a better place. Now I'm wondering if I'm part of the problem.

From here I have three options. I can:

1. Bury my head in the sand and pretend the 'Mind the Hype' debate isn't happening.
2. Metamorphose into a cynic and declare that we can't trust anyone, not even scientists. Or,
3. Put my critical thinking journalistic hat firmly back on and keep asking questions.

Back in 2013, after years of being disappointed by both the mainstream and alternative treatment paths for my autoimmune disease, I decided that I needed to apply the same journalistic rigour that I used in my day job to my health. In other words, I learned how to be a health sceptic.

Not to be confused with being a cynic, the word sceptic is derived from Ancient Greek verbs such as 'skeptikos' or 'skeptomai' which mean variations of 'to search', 'to examine', 'to think', or 'to look for'. When it came to my health, being a modern-day sceptic meant learning how to think like a scientist and to view the world through a lens of objectivity in order to try to see things clearly. This also meant looking at the available evidence and coming to conclusions that are supported and verifiable. Most importantly, though, being a sceptical journalist meant embracing the possibility of being proven wrong and relishing the chance to follow a story to its logical end. Of the choices I now face during my professional crisis, I'm choosing option three. I'm going to keep asking questions.

I decided to get in touch with the lead author of the 'Mind the Hype' paper, Nicholas Van Dam. It turns out the American researcher recently married an Aussie and is now a Senior Lecturer in Clinical Psychology and Deputy Director of the Brain and Mental Health Hub at the University of Melbourne. I was due to fly to Melbourne for my next EEG brain scans anyhow, so we caught up for lunch in the food capital of Australia.

Over a bowl of noodles, I shouldn't have been surprised to learn that the headlines generated by Nicholas's paper were exaggerated. 'The main story we want to convey is that there's this idea, or sentiment, that mindfulness can be used as a solution, or treatment, or a fix for just about anything and there's been this massive growth in the marketisation of this idea,' he said. 'And one of the things that I often teach when I'm training clinical psychology students how to do psychotherapy, is that if someone tells you that a new intervention will fix everything, then ask them hard questions, because anyone who's trying to tell you that one thing works for 100 per cent of the time for 100 per cent of the people is not telling you the whole story.'

As Nicholas talked I started to understand that his main message is not that mindfulness is bunk but that the public appetite for it is outpacing the speed of the evidence. It's not that there aren't good studies being published, or that mindfulness doesn't hold promise, but rather that there is still a lot more research to do.

When I thought about it, what Nicholas said made perfect sense in the context of the evidence-based recommendations we now have on things like how much sleep we should be getting, what foods we should (and shouldn't) be eating, and how much exercise we should be doing.

ROUGH TIMELINE OF HEALTH RESEARCH

1880s	1910s	1950s	2010s
EXERCISE	NUTRITION	SLEEP	MEDITATION
Exercise laboratories established	Discovery of vitamins	Discovery of REM sleep	MRIs became more widely available

In order to gauge where we're actually up to with mindfulness research in the context of other promising mental health interventions, I did a search to compare the number of studies that have been done on using mindfulness for depression with the number of studies that have been done on using diet for depression. I looked for randomised controlled trials, which are considered the gold standard of science, as well as meta-analysis papers, which offer a kind of big-picture view on what the science is showing.

When scientists did a meta-analysis on studies that examined the effects of improved diet on depression symptoms, they had a pool of 16 eligible randomised controlled trials to include, involving a total of 45826 participants.[13] In line with

DIET & DEPRESSION META-ANALYSIS VS MINDFULNESS & DEPRESSION META-ANALYSIS

No. of people = 45 826 VS No. of people = 1341

Firth J, Marx W, Dash S, et al. The Effects of Dietary Improvement on Symptoms of Depression and Anxiety: A Meta-Analysis of Randomized Controlled Trials. Psychosom Med. 2019; 81(3): 265-280.

conventional wisdom, the results concluded that 'dietary interventions hold promise as a novel intervention for reducing symptoms of depression'. When scientists did a meta-analysis to see if mindfulness training improves symptoms of depression and anxiety, they concluded that, yes, the 'regular performance of mindfulness exercises is beneficial'. But although they had 18 studies to work with, only *some* were of the gold-standard variety, and in total there were only 1341 participants.[14]

This tells me that it's very early days for the science of mindfulness, that I need to be really careful about how I report the evidence, and that researchers still have a lot of work to do in order to investigate when, why, how and for whom mindfulness can be effective.

Buyer Beware

This story is turning out to be a tale of nuance and subtlety, and if my longitudinal investigation is going to reveal anything, I need to keep asking the hard questions, no matter how uncomfortable the answers may be. This commitment has led me to get in touch with another author on the 'Mind the Hype' paper, Associate Professor Willoughby Britton from Brown University, who has recently attracted a lot of attention for her research investigating the good, the bad and the banal effects of contemplative practice. Willoughby is a clinical psychologist and Ivy League scientist who has been meditating for 25 years. When neuroscientists study expert meditators who have done more than 10 000 hours of practice, they use brains like hers. She is also a meditation teacher who has trained in Mindfulness

Based Stress Reduction (MBSR) and Mindfulness Based Cognitive Therapy (MBCT).

In 2006, she was doing her psychiatric internship at an inpatient hospital when two people who had been at a 10-day mindfulness meditation retreat centre were admitted. At a time when mindfulness was being widely promoted for its stress-busting, wellbeing-boosting powers of emotional stability and inner calm, it seemed to her like an important topic to follow up.

After establishing herself as a clinical researcher at Brown, in 2015 Willoughby and her team published the 'Varieties of Contemplative Experience' study which, rather than tracking the positive outcomes of mindfulness training, interviewed almost 100 meditation teachers and students about their challenging experiences.[15] The aim was to highlight that practising mindfulness is not always all warm and fuzzy, and to document the full range of meditation-induced outcomes.

The results were revealing. Meditators reported everything from hypersensitivity to light or sound, insomnia, both heightened and dampened emotions, increased fear, anxiety and flashback trauma, and even losing a sense of self. 'Probably one of the most common problems is people saying, "I don't feel like I exist", or "I don't know how I'm going to function tomorrow", or "I don't feel anything for the people that I know",' Willoughby – who now receives regular calls from distressed meditators – told me.

Although I haven't been experiencing excessive levels of anxiety or flashbacks, and my sense of self remains intact, it's a relief to know that I'm not alone in finding meditation challenging and sometimes stressful. During my practice, my mental experience can drift from work and finance worry to family worry, then from worrying about others to worrying about what others think of my actions. I might mentally time travel to an imagined catastrophic future or ruminate on painful things that I've tried to forget. And if it's not emotional pain that worries me, it can be physical pain that dominates my awareness. As if all that weren't enough to worry about, I also sometimes get caught up in worrying about worrying.

Fortunately, I've seen psychologists in the past who have given me the skills to recognise when I'm really struggling and in need of professional help, but I can see why Willoughby is concerned that there is currently no widely accepted international accreditation organisation for mindfulness teachers or products.

Researchers don't yet have enough data to be able to recommend specific meditation techniques, in specific doses, to specific people for specific purposes. So, for that, and for now, we'll have to rely on the guidance of qualified and experienced teachers and efforts to establish mindfulness meditation teaching standards have been under way for more than a decade around the world.[16] But exactly what those standards should be, how they should be quantified, and who should enforce them is up for debate.

Although Willoughby doesn't think meditation teachers should be required to have a degree in clinical psychology, she's convinced they should at least have basic mental health first aid training. 'It's important, especially if meditation practices are being used to treat mental health issues, that meditation teachers are able to identify some basic issues and know what to do about it,' she said.

In addition to providing counselling for distressed meditators, Willoughby's charitable organisation, Cheetah House, also works with teacher organisations to create meditation safety plans and training programs, and her message is starting to cut through the noise. Many of the leading mindfulness organisations and associations have taken up her three-day 'First Do No Harm Meditation Safety' program and are increasingly demanding more rigorous criteria for registered teachers.

Based on my own meditation experiences so far, if not for the fact that I've been talking to experts, at this point in my mindful experiment I'd probably be calling it a day. Sticking to something this unpleasant just doesn't seem worth it.

In order to work through my struggles I called Sydney-based teacher and clinical psychologist Timothea (Tim) Goddard, with whom I'll be doing an MBSR course in a few weeks' time. Tim assured me that all this is totally normal, expected, and kind of the point. 'I don't want to be glib or flippant about the real need for us to be so onto it, especially trauma-sensitive stuff, but mindfulness meditation is going to be full of adverse events because we're inviting contemplation of our own inner life and outer life, and there's going to be a lot of adverse stuff in there. People are going to feel their pain, their sadness, their grief, their inability to be the person they want to be. They're going to feel shame. And I would argue that that's what it's for. It's actually good for us to be able to process and make a different relationship with these

things and to know that we are whole, even with those things going on,' she explained over the phone.

I understand why Herbert Benson and Jon Kabat-Zinn originally labelled mindfulness as being for 'stress reduction' rather than something like 'experiential awareness training'. They were coming hot on the heels of Hans Selye, the so-called 'father of stress' and founder of the stress theory, who was nominated for the Nobel Prize 17 times for his work on stress and health. (I was stunned when it was recently revealed that Selye was funded by Big Tobacco because his research findings aided the marketability of cigarettes as a stress reduction tool.[17]) Back then, when stress was first being marketed as a *problem*, there would have been a cultural necessity for the therapeutic benefits of the opposite of stress, *relaxation*. The promise of stress reduction would certainly have got people through the meditation school doors.

These days we probably feel we need stress busters more than ever, but the realisation that mindfulness is actually first and foremost about becoming aware of whatever is happening (good, bad, and everything in between) makes me think that it might need a 21st century rebrand. After just a few weeks of practising mindfulness every day, I can already tell that stress reduction isn't quite what mindfulness is and does. Mindfulness training *can* be relaxing. But it can also be difficult. Mindfulness training *can* reduce stress. But it can also make me aware of how stressed I am, and without guidance from a good teacher that could be *really* stressful.

Willoughby's research offers an interesting hint as to a possible way to keep at this despite my resistance. The subjects in the 'Variety of Contemplative Experiences' study also reported a range of different emotional *reactions* to their challenging experiences, from neutral curiosity to bliss and joy, fear and terror. This makes me think that in the same way that one person might view the end of their marriage as a heartbreak that sets off a downward emotional spiral, another may see it as a break*through* and new beginning.

There is something to this idea that the way we interpret or perceive things might be a critical piece of the puzzle and I'm making a note to investigate this further. I'm also going to start working on my own perception of my meditation experience. I'll see if I can work *with* my discomfort and unpleasant experiences instead of constantly resisting them. It will be interesting to see if I can change how I feel and what, if anything, happens as a result.

'So is my year of living mindfully a waste of time?' I hesitantly asked Nicholas Van Dam, not quite sure if I wanted to know his answer before I headed off to a lab at Monash University, where neuroscientist Neil Bailey would be using an electroencephalogram (EEG) to scan my brain.

'The biggest limitation is that it's hard to know whether or not the findings that you would get from one person will tell you anything about a different person. Essentially, with one person we just can't draw that conclusion that it will generalise to everyone … but that's not to say it's worthless. There are lots of case studies out there and case studies are often really important starts. In most scientific fields, particularly in the applied sciences, in medicine, we often start with case studies,' he said, before encouraging me to keep going.

I began this project believing in evidence. I lined up 18 interviews with top scientists and signed up for every test I could think of. But I'm starting to realise that I'm going to have to get comfortable with the incomplete, imperfect nature of our knowledge, and that objective black and white data might not tell the whole story.

At the end of my first month meditating every day there is one thing I know for sure: no matter how many products on Amazon might suggest otherwise, you simply can't *buy* mindfulness. If Matthieu Ricard's version of caring mindfulness is a skill, it will only be learned through hours of uncomfortable contemplation.

CHAPTER THREE

It's *Not* the Thought That Counts

On the Case

In my student days at the University of Technology in Sydney (UTS) my journalism professor, Peter Manning, used to say that being a good investigative journalist meant carrying out in-depth, multifaceted explorations of complex issues in their real-life settings and then presenting the story as though the whole endeavour were a piece of cake. As someone who naturally loved asking questions and finding answers, who enjoyed the process of investigation just as much as the result, and someone who valued truth and fairness, I was hooked.

I don't know how this particular investigative deep dive will turn out, but my foray into the 'Mind the Hype' discussion tells me that the science component may not be the signature ingredient after all. I've decided to go back to journalism 101 – which means that in addition to continuing to delve into the research, interviewing people, and maintaining my own meditation practice, I also need to find some case studies.

Case studies are often dismissed as anecdotal, but historically they've played an important role in psychological research, clinical medicine and scientific breakthroughs. Although findings on a single case study cannot be generalised, they nevertheless provide an up-close, in-depth and detailed investigation of a subject, in a real-life context, and this is an invaluable tool for either supporting or disproving burgeoning theories, and for framing questions for more rigorously designed clinical studies. Just as Josef Breuer and Sigmund Freud laid the foundations for psychoanalysis when they documented their experimental treatments of 'Anna O', and just as physician and vaccination pioneer Edward Jenner proved the ability to vaccinate against smallpox by demonstrating its effectiveness in an eight-year-old boy[1], I'm now wondering if there are any mindfulness equivalents. There must be good reasons that millions of people around the world have added mindfulness to their daily To Do lists.

This line of thinking led me to the set of *Good Morning America* in New York City, awaiting ABC News journalist Dan Harris to finish work for the day. Dan had just flown in from Russia, where he was reporting for *Nightline* on the troll farms that are thought to have played a role in the outcome of the 2016 US presidential election. As the face of both weekend *GMA*, which airs at 8.00 a.m., and *Nightline* during the week, which airs at 11.00 p.m., he'd been awake since four in the morning and had only had a few hours' sleep. Despite his relentless schedule, jet lag and having a terrible head cold, he made time to be my first case study.

CASE STUDY #1 – PART 1

Dan Harris – ABC News journalist and founder of the Ten Percent Happier mindfulness app
[Edited transcript]

Me: Let's start at the beginning: how many people saw you lose your mind on national television?

Dan: 5.019 million – according to the Nielsen Ratings.

Me: Tell me about what led to your on-air panic attack.

Dan: I started in television news when I was 22 and when I was 28 I got a job at ABC News. Shortly after I arrived 9/11 happened and I ended up spending a lot of time in Afghanistan, Pakistan, Israel, the West Bank – Gaza. I went to Iraq six times and I didn't spend a lot of time thinking about what the psychological consequences might be, and so when I came home I kind of bottomed out. I got depressed, although I didn't even know I was depressed. I was having trouble getting out of bed, I felt like I had a low-grade fever all the time. I went and consulted a bunch of doctors, and before I actually got a diagnosis of depression I did something very dumb, which was I started to self-medicate with recreational drugs including cocaine and ecstasy.

Me: When did things start to change?

Dan: The bottom for me was freaking out on national television. June 2004, I was reading the headlines. My lungs seized up, my heart was racing. I just couldn't talk, which is a problem when talking is what you need to do for a living.

And it's a vicious cycle between the thinking and the physical manifestations. So your body starts to mutiny and your mind picks up on that obviously and is like, 'What the fuck is this?' You start thinking, 'Oh my God, I'm freaking out, I'm having a panic attack, and I'm on national television.' And then the body reacts to all of that and starts freaking out even more. The fight-or-flight response was useful when we were being chased by sabre-tooth tigers, but in a modern context, we're both the person being chased by a tiger *and* the tiger. You know, we're doing it to ourselves.

Medicine's Poor Cousin

Like many people before him, Dan used his rock bottom to start swimming towards recovery. I'm using his story as a beginning point for my own exploration into how mindfulness training might benefit people with mental illnesses such as depression.

For all our scientific, technological and medical breakthroughs, at a time when approximately 300 million people have depression and every 40 seconds someone, somewhere, takes their own life, there's something wrong with our current mainstream approach, which separates our mind from our body, and our psychological from our physical wellbeing.[2-4]

In order to tackle this woefully underreported issue I got in touch with Professor Willem Kuyken, the Director of the University of Oxford Mindfulness Centre, who is at the forefront of finding evidence-based approaches to depression. Willem was recently listed among the 'Who's Who' of influential

MENTAL HEALTH STATS THAT STUN ME:

50%

The percentage of people with depression who don't get any treatment

---

30%

The percentage of people who have treatment - resistant depression

---

1:1,000,000

The ratio of psychiatrists per population in over half the countries in the world researchers because his papers investigating mindfulness and depression have ranked him in the top one per cent of researchers cited in his field.[5]

Over a video connection from his office at the Oxford Mindfulness Centre, where he's just launched the world's first project investigating if mindfulness training in teenagers can prevent depression later in life, Willem told me that he's especially concerned by the fact that there is a 50 per cent chance that if you've had depression once you will get it again, and an 80 per cent chance that if you've had depression twice, you will get it a third time.[6] 'If you think about depression as a recurrent problem, that means it's a one-billion person problem; a billion people will suffer depression at some point in their lifetime,' he said.

As someone with a childhood memory of the heart-rending consequences of depression and suicide, I find this alarming. Depression is an illness that not only affects how a person feels, thinks, and behaves; it affects their entire family too.

There's also the link between mental and physical health. People who have depression are more likely to have other health problems and people who have chronic illnesses are more likely to be depressed. In fact, people with severe and prolonged mental illness are at risk of dying on average 15 to 20 years earlier than other people, and people with long-term illnesses suffer more complications if they also develop mental health problems, increasing the cost of care by an average of 45 per cent.[7]

And yet, despite the compelling case to urgently elevate the status of mental wellbeing in healthcare and society, psychological health research has long been the poor cousin of medical science. For example, in the UK, a country considered

	Cancer Research VS. Funding	Mental Health Research Funding
No. of people affected	2.7 million	13.4 million
£ spent on research	611.7 million	124.3 million

*Source – MQ: Transforming Mental Health. UK Mental Health Research Funding, 2019.

to have one of the best health systems in the world, they spend 25 times more per capita on cancer research than on mental health research.[8]

It's not that I think one form of research is more important than the other, but when the impact of mental illness on UK health services, as well as in lost productivity and reduced quality of life, comes with a £105.2 billion price tag, the lack of funding seems nonsensical.[9]

It's true that public attitudes towards mental health are improving and there is increasing commitment from workplaces, medical systems, schools and within government to change, but current prevention and treatment options are still relatively limited. 'People can talk about it, but that talk has to go somewhere. It has to turn into something that actually makes a difference to people's lives,' said Willem.

He believes that we need to shift our approach and start thinking of our mental health as being on a continuum from excellent to terminal. Currently, we wait until people are already really unwell before offering any help. 'It's like we're waiting for the cancer to be at stage three or four before intervening,' he said.

As he talked I couldn't help but think about my own predicament when I started this mindfulness project. I'd rated myself just below average on the Mental Health Continuum that was developed by Professor Corey Keyes, from Emory University, but I felt almost embarrassed that I might need an intervention, as if because I wasn't in a full-blown crisis I shouldn't need to be doing anything.

Against this backdrop, mindfulness, which can be delivered in a group format, practised at home, and can work as an adjunct to whatever else is available, is worth investigating. In particular, a program called Mindfulness Based Cognitive Therapy (MBCT) is currently being picked apart by scientists wanting to understand the 'how', 'why' and 'for whom' of mindfulness and depression.

MBCT combines elements of Jon Kabat-Zinn's Mindfulness Based Stress Reduction (MBSR) with Cognitive Behaviour Therapy (CBT), which was developed by Aaron Beck in the 1960s and aims to help people change their distorted, damaging thinking and behaviour.

'People at risk of depression are dealing with a lot of negative thoughts, feelings and beliefs about themselves,' explained Willem, who in addition to decades of mindfulness training also studied CBT as a Postdoctoral Fellow at the University of Pennsylvania with Beck. 'A sad mood or negative thinking can be very powerful and potent. Just a small negative thought can very quickly turn into a downward spiral of depressive thinking, withdrawal and depressive relapse.'

The research so far is encouraging. Willem recently co-authored a meta-analysis (a study of studies involving a total of 1258 participants) which demonstrated that MBCT is as equally effective as anti-depressant medication for preventing relapsing depression.[10] Although the 10 studies included represent a relatively small number of the gold-standard studies, this is a noteworthy start considering that MBCT has only been around for 15 or so years, whereas medication for depression has been studied since the 1950s.[11]

Based on my own fledgling mindfulness practice, I suspect that mindfulness training may work on a number of psychological levels (attention control, personal awareness, body awareness, emotion regulation, and so forth) but Willem explained that the central mechanism underpinning how MBCT works is known as 'decentering', which is science-speak for becoming aware of incoming thoughts and feelings and accepting them, but not attaching or reacting to them.[12] 'When people at risk of depression learn mindfulness, they come to see that negative thoughts, negative feelings and negative memories are a bit like weather patterns. Instead of getting caught up and carried away by them, they can just see them coming through and passing through awareness.'

Uncovering the 'how' of MBCT also interests Willoughby Britton, the clinical psychologist and researcher at Brown University whom I originally spoke to about the potential adverse effects of mindfulness training. In one study, Willoughby and her team asked 52 people with partially remitted depression to either take part in an MBCT course, or to sit on a wait list that would delay the start of their MBCT course until after the study. Both groups agreed to a three-hour laboratory-based ordeal that included the Trier Social Stress Test, which involves having to give a spontaneous speech to a panel of hostile judges and has been shown to raise our levels of the stress hormone, cortisol, by a whopping 300 per cent.[13]

The results were intriguing. Emotionally and physiologically, the group that had been taught MBCT recovered from their nightmarish speech experience faster. 'The control group that had been on the wait list were probably still thinking, "That was the *worst* experience *ever*", and really ruminating about it, whereas the mindfulness group had learned to let go of that and they came back to baseline much faster,' Willoughby explained.

This 'decentering' mechanism fits hand in glove with what Dan Harris described.

CASE STUDY #1 – PART 2

**Dan Harris – ABC News journalist and founder of
the Ten Percent Happier mindfulness app**

[Edited transcript]

Dan: I came home one night and my wife gave me a book by a guy named Dr Mark Epstein, who I liked right away because he had actual credentials, as opposed to some of these self-help folk who don't, to put it kindly. Epstein writes about the overlap

---

between psychology and Buddhism, and it was this very dry-eyed, commonsense diagnosis of the human situation.

The Buddha has this term – 'the monkey mind' – where we hurl ourselves from one hit of pleasant experience, one movie, one vacation, one latte to the next, and yet are never fully satisfied. The Buddha's description of the human situation was very compelling, his prescription was repellent, which was that he says you should meditate. I did not want to do that. I thought it was ridiculous and that meditation was for people who were into crystals and Kombucha and Enya. But for me, what changed my mind was reading about the science.

It was a couple of weeks before I started noticing some differences. The biggest one was mindfulness. We spend so much of our time just being yanked around by the malevolent puppeteer of our ego. Some neurotic thought or obsession pops into our head, you know, 'I need a sleeve of Oreos', or 'I need to say the thing that will fuck up the next 48 hours of my marriage' … and we just do it. There's no buffer between the stimulus and our blind reaction.

Mindfulness is like this inner meteorologist that can see and go, 'Yeah, there's a hurricane about to hit and I don't need to get carried away by it automatically, reflexively, habitually. I have some choice.'

I'm still the same person, right. So I still have a predisposition toward depression, anxiety, panic and substance abuse. I can still sometimes feel the low cloud ceiling of depression once in a while, but I'm less likely to believe the bullshit that the ego coughs up. So what could be a several-day-long trudge through mopeyness and despair actually can be truncated quite dramatically to a couple of hours, a couple of minutes, who knows.

Me: Does the critical thinking journalist in you ever worry if you've just bought massively into a cult?

Dan: I called my book *10% Happier* for a reason. If my book was called *Be Happy Now* or *This Is the Solution to All of Your Problems*, then yeah, I'd worry about that. But I think the vast swath of humanity could benefit from this very simple thing of just sitting down, closing your eyes, or not, trying to feel your breath coming in and going out, and when you get distracted start again and again. The lessons there from this really simple little thing are incredibly rich.

Sweet Surrender

I'm halfway through the third month of my experiment and even with just 20 minutes of practising a body scan meditation each day, I'm starting to understand what Dan was talking about when he described 'unshackling' from his automatic thoughts. It feels as though something is shifting. I'm getting better at decentering – objectively noticing the crazy, busy, hectic, automatic thoughts that circle around in my head again and again, and I'm especially catching these thinking loops as they kick off before I go to bed. This, according to Judson (Jud) Brewer, a neuroscientist and the director of research and innovation at the Mindfulness Center at Brown University, is exactly what the training is supposed to be teaching me.

Among other things, Jud is also an addiction psychiatrist who's developing and evaluating app-delivered mindfulness programs for smoking, anxiety and emotional eating. Over a video call from Providence, Rhode Island, he explained that understanding how our minds work to cause things like depression, anxiety, rumination and insomnia is essential for the next phase of mental health research. 'If I was developing a pill to help people lower their blood pressure, I would want to understand how people's blood pressure is rising in the first place, so that I could design a pill specifically for that. I'd love to see more training programs developed specifically grounded in the mechanisms of how the mind works, and how mindfulness is directly targeting those mechanistic pathways,' he said.

I've suffered from insomnia on and off since I was a teenager, and it's not surprising that having a tendency to ruminate has been identified as a contributing factor.[14] I recently went over some notes I made in the early hours of the morning shortly before this experiment began.

Though the hours between dusk and dawn seem lonely, I'm far from alone in my sleep difficulties. It's estimated that around 40 per cent of the population have trouble getting to sleep or staying asleep at some stage in their lives. This warrants consideration because lost sleep is linked with a host of chronic diseases such as anxiety, depression, fibromyalgia, diabetes, epilepsy and Parkinson's disease.[15,16] With research indicating that poor sleep may not only have been one of the causes of my autoimmune disease, but that it also exacerbates my symptoms, I know I need to get better at getting to sleep.[16,17]

MEDITATION JOURNAL, DAY 28

The day is done but my mind is not. It's 2.23 a.m. and while the whole world slumbers, I am at war. No matter how I fluff my pillow or stuff my quilt exactly right, I toss and turn. I cannot sleep. Resistance is futile against the relentless tide of thoughts which come of their own volition. They say I'm a failure. A fool. They say I should fear for my health, worry for my children. They speak of remembered pain and imagined future grief. They tell me I'll be a wreck when the morning comes. They trap me. Ensnare me. I am caught in their web and I cannot get out. Under the spell of restless wakeful semiconsciousness, I am losing my mind.

I've spent years trying to improve my sleep and taken advantage of my job title to seek advice from some of the world's leading sleep researchers. On their recommendations, I've established a rather elaborate bedtime routine, which among other things includes blue-light blocking glasses if I watch television after sundown, block-out blinds in my bedroom, and red-tinted globes in my night lamps.

Even with these 'sleep hygiene' rituals in place, sometimes I have a miserable night because of forces beyond my control: it may be that little Isaac, who's still learning how to resettle himself after he wakes in the night, might need my help, or that I've had too much caffeine earlier in the day; but more often than not, when I'm still up at 2.23 a.m. it's not because of external forces, it's because of a battle that rages within me.

'So my patients come into my office and they say, "Doc, I can't sleep," and I say, okay, tell me if this is what's happening

… You lay down on the pillow and your head says, "My turn," and it starts looping and saying, "Oh, I can't believe I did this or that," or "What about that thing at work?" or, "How am I gonna be able to do this or that next week?" and then you can't get to sleep. Then, when you look at the clock, your brain says, "Oh, I can't get to sleep, now I'm gonna be sleepy tomorrow," and then it just goes on and on and on,' said Jud, who had just described my own night-time misery with eerie accuracy.

According to Jud, when I have worrying thoughts, my brain can seek relief from its discomfort by trying to solve a problem, but when the problem isn't being solved, it can trigger more worrying thoughts, which my brain then tries to solve. The loop can continue on and on in an endless cycle of futile, ruminative, non-problem solving, even when what I really want and need is to get some zzzs. I'm currently road testing his Unwinding Anxiety app and, to my surprise, I'm finding that it's putting me to sleep …

MEDITATION JOURNAL, DAY 72

Time: *20 minutes daily*

Method: *Unwinding Anxiety app*

Technique: *20-minute body scan meditation led by Judson Brewer MD, PhD*

Experiment notes:

Jud is telling me to bring a curious kind of awareness to my left toes. Geez it's hot tonight. Now to the bottom of my left

---

foot. It's too hot to be using this blanket. Now to the top of my left foot … I should have replied to that email about the interview next week before I lay down in bed. What if it's too late to set it up? Oh, here we go, thoughts kicking off. I'll probably be up all night now. Oh, right, thinking about email. Back to my left foot. Left ankle. Left knee. I quite like this body scan technique. The systematic progression of body awareness makes me able to better concentrate and realise when I'm off track and distracted. Wait, did Jud skip my left thigh or was I distracted? Moving my attention up to my left hip. Left side. Left arm. Jud tells me to think of my awareness as a spotlight moving slowly through my body … Bring my attention to my abdomen. Rising. Falling. Bring my attention to my chest. Rising. Falling. I can feel my body on the mattress … My heavy neck … My tired eyes … Drifting … drifting … drifting. Zzzzzzzzzz.

Part of me wonders if it's all a placebo, but since I've been practising Jud's body scan technique before bed, I haven't had insomnia in weeks. 'Before you started meditating, what was your insomnia like?' Jud asked me during our video call.

'Once or twice a week I would be going through the night, unable to sleep,' I replied.

'And your mind racing, you know thoughts, thoughts, thoughts, thoughts?' he asked.

'Exactly,' I replied.

'One of the simplest things I give to my patients who have clinical insomnia is the body scan. So what are you noticing with mindfulness, are you able to notice that worry thinking and then let go of it, or is it not even coming up?' he asked.

'I'm really aware, like, "Oh my God, I've got all these anxious thoughts" and so before I'm going to bed I'm kind of mitigating my behaviour so I don't go to bed ruminating,' I said.

'How is that placebo? What you're describing is an actual behaviour change, catching that worry thinking, not feeding it and by not feeding it, not having insomnia. So you can see a causal link there.'

Interestingly, I'm finding physical relaxation naturally follows the relaxation of my mental load. It's as if when my mind relaxes, my muscles can follow suit and more often than not so too does blessed, blessed sleep.[18]

When Jud explained this process so simply, I could see why the research on mindfulness for insomnia has so much potential. A recent review of six randomised controlled trials that put high-quality mindfulness-based interventions for insomnia to the test demonstrated significant benefits.[19] One pilot study compared medication and meditation and found them to be comparably effective, which is good news for someone like me who experiences foggy-headed daytime side effects from sleep medication.[20]

I'm not under any illusion that mindfulness training is the cure-all for the world's sleep problems; the causes of my sleeplessness and the sleeplessness of other people are complicated. (I recently spoke to a light-sleeping long-term meditator whose problem is not falling asleep but rather *staying* asleep, and I know other people are genetically programmed to wake extremely early or not feel sleepy until it's extraordinarily late.) But for this very tired mother who could use all the sleep she can get, learning to decentre – to view my thoughts from a distance and to know that it's *not* actually the thought that counts – could be a missing link in my lifelong battle against insomnia.

SIX MECHANISMS OF MINDFULNESS

It is remarkable that after decades of psychotherapy research, we can not provide an evidence-based explanation for how or why even our most well studied interventions produce change.

– Professor Alan Kazdin, Annual Review of
Clinical Psychology, 2007[21]

Researchers have made great efforts since 2007, when Sterling Professor Emeritus of Psychology at Yale University Alan Kazdin wrote those daunting words about the state of psychological research. Although we know that mindfulness training can have an effect on things such as brain function and structure, one of the most important unanswered questions remains: how does it work? Discovering the *how* gives us a greater ability to distil the active ingredients and therefore make the practice, the programs and the treatments more powerful.

To keep track, I've created myself a glossary of 'mechanisms of mindfulness' that I'm frequently coming across in scientific papers.

1. Attention Control
Especially in the beginning, mindfulness involves cultivating the ability to control my attention. I'm training to detect when

---

my mind is wandering and to then reorientate my mental focus to my original target of concentration.[22] Attention is important because it can shape my experience and perspective.[23] I suspect improving this skill will be very helpful in a world so cluttered with distraction.[24]

2. Emotion Regulation

Emotion regulation is a core psychological process thought to be critical for maintaining wellbeing.[25] There is a range of different strategies (some that I'm not even consciously aware I'm doing) that I can use to increase, maintain or decrease my emotional response.[26] For example, I might re-appraise a situation (*I really screwed up that interview, what a great learning experience*) or I might suppress how I'm feeling (*I'm infuriated about this email! Wait, take a deep breath before responding*).[27] Generally, the view is that 'mindful emotion regulation' is a unique strategy that works on multiple levels, including evaluating, expressing and experiencing aspects of emotion.[28–30] Mindfulness teaches me to become aware of my mental state then change my relationship to it.[31,32] Instead of getting caught up, I'm able to take a step back and become less emotionally invested, which in turn enables me to self-regulate, clarify my values, and respond rather than react.[32]

3. Decentering

This is about developing the ability to 'step outside' of my immediate experience, thereby changing the very nature of that experience.[33] Developing an ability to observe my thoughts

and feelings as temporary and automatic 'events' in my mind
rather than 'facts' or true descriptions of reality is necessary
for mental health and development, whereas the absence
of this ability is thought to lead to psychological and social
dysfunction.[34] Decentering entails three similar and interrelated
processes: *'meta-awareness', 'disidentification',* and *'reduced reactivity to
thought content'*.[35] The basic idea is to learn a distinction between
thinking and believing a thought and being meta-aware of and
noting the thought (*I am worthless* vs *huh, a self critical thought*).[35–37]
Through mindfulness I'm cultivating the ability to step back
and perceive my inner experiences as transient, momentary
occurrences rather than 'who I am'. For example, the thought,
'Oh no, she doesn't like me', will not necessarily spark anxiety
or rumination during or after a social interaction.[35] This
mechanism enables me to be less reactive to the contents of my
mind.

4. Acceptance

One of the ideas behind mindfulness training is to notice
and allow all my experiences (even difficult or stressful ones)
to arise and pass without further elaboration, evaluation, or
reactivity.[38] Accepting my negative mental experiences in
particular is considered a key mechanism explaining how and
why mindfulness might improve my psychological wellbeing.
Acceptance can have a kind of blunting effect on my emotional
reactions to bad experiences which can, over time, lead to
improved wellbeing.[39] I have a feeling that learning the skill
of acceptance is going to help me avoid a lot of unnecessary

suffering during life's unavoidable difficult moments, from toddler tantrums in supermarkets to handling jerks at work. To be clear, this is not about becoming a doormat when bad things happen but, rather, about a particular vantage point that allows me to ponder difficulties with discernment and, hopefully, wisdom.

5. Interoceptive awareness

This is about learning to notice, access and appraise my inner body sensations.[40] In a nutshell, it's thought that sensations in my body play an essential role in my cognition: that is, knowing things, perceiving the world and making interpretations.[41] It is my interoception that drives my behaviour. When I feel hunger sensations I know I should eat. When I feel sleepy I know I should go to bed. In addition, interoceptive awareness is critical for decision-making, flexible thinking, social awareness and emotional intelligence. This is known as 'embodied cognition' and linked to the origin of consciousness itself. Some researchers argue that this might be *the* most important of all the mechanisms and that mindfulness training may even be better described simply as 'increased interoception'.[42] Having poor interoceptive awareness is linked to mental illness. For example, people with major depressive disorder are less able to sense their own heartbeat.[43]

6. Self-transcendence

This one is the hardest mechanisms to grasp. Apparently as I get more experienced, mindfulness may not only help to develop self-awareness, but it may also enable me to *transcend* the sense of there being a separate 'self' from everything else. That is, dissolve distinctions between myself and other.[44] Developing a felt-sense that everything is connected to everything else may result in feeling more supported and more prosocial, and acting more compassionately, and thus create a greater sense of wellbeing. Hopefully, as I progress in my year, this mechanism will make more sense.[44]

Seeking Serenity

If suffering brings wisdom, I would wish to be less wise.

– From *Mosada*, a short verse play in three scenes written by William Butler Yeats, published in 1886[45]

Jud's mission to try to pin down the 'neuro-signature' of mindfulness training has led him to begin identifying brain networks associated with this 'getting caught up' vs 'stepping back' decentering training that I'm doing. And this not only has implications for chronic ruminators like me, but also for treating craving and addiction.

'Mechanistically, it seems that mindfulness is helping to decouple the craving and the behaviour, so that piece [of evidence] we've seen multiple times in our lab. Where we might be able to start applying this is to other types of behaviours, whether it's smoking cigarettes, drinking alcohol, smoking crack cocaine, using heroin, eating food, or even going on social media, these behaviours have all been shown to activate the same brain systems as known drugs of abuse,' Jud explained before telling me about one of his studies that demonstrated that four weeks of mindfulness training was five times more successful than a gold-standard program designed to help people to quit smoking.[46]

'Sorry, Jud, you got five times the quit rates of gold-standard treatments?' I couldn't help but interrupt him, knowing that tobacco is regularly cited as one of the most difficult drugs to quit, and thought to be on par with or even more difficult than getting off heroin.[47]

'Yes, we found that they were five times more likely to have quit smoking than gold-standard treatment [programs] and mechanistically we could see how the mindfulness training was decoupling the craving for cigarettes from the behaviour of smoking,' he said.

Jud's work comes at a crucial time for addiction research. Approximately 31 million people around the world are problematic drug users, meaning that their drug use is harmful to the point where they need treatment.[48] In the US, this comes with a $740 billion annual price tag because of related crime, loss of work productivity, and healthcare costs.[49]

Having grown up with three people close to me who suffered from various substance abuse disorders including drugs and alcohol, the importance of Jud's research is personal. Loving an addict comes with the wretched knowledge that they are more likely to fail in their efforts to quit than succeed. Overcoming addiction is complicated and difficult and sometimes seemingly impossible. And despite there being a number of evidence-based treatment options, relapse rates are as high as 60 per cent in the year following treatment.[50,51]

Although there's a lot more work to be done by Jud and his addiction research colleagues, a meta-analysis on mindfulness interventions for addiction concluded that, to varying degrees, mindfulness can have significant effects in reducing the frequency and severity of substance misuse, the intensity of craving, and the severity of stress.[52] Another review found that mindfulness-based interventions were associated with reduced consumption of alcohol, cocaine, amphetamines, marijuana and opiates.[53]

In my youth, I couldn't understand why people I loved just couldn't stop. As I patched up their wounds, cleaned up the mess, repeatedly researched the 'best' rehab programs, and bore witness to their desperate moments of crisis; did they not care how their behaviour was impacting others? Couldn't they use more willpower? For the sake of themselves and everyone around them, why couldn't they just … *quit?*

Now, as an adult, I understand that their troubles were not driven by a fundamental personality flaw, a lack of self-control, or some sort of selfish drive to pursue hedonistic pleasure at any cost. Drug and alcohol use are often the result of a neglected mental life; of a desire to escape shame, grief, abandonment and pain. Addiction doesn't just happen to people because they come across a particularly pleasant mind-altering chemical and begin taking it regularly. It's a maladaptive way of coping, borne from the simple desire to seek relief from suffering.

By helping people to accept their problems for what they are and to recognise their triggers, perhaps this is how mindfulness works to help people with addictions more skilfully ride out their cravings. And perhaps this is a clue as to why mindfulness, which works as an adjunct to the best of other treatments available, is gaining broad acceptance among mental health professionals.

CHAPTER FOUR

Mindful Medicine

Let us keep our minds open, by all means, as long as that means keeping our sense of perspective and seeking an understanding of the forces which mould the world. But don't keep your minds so open that your brains fall out!

Excerpt from a speech given by Walter Kotschnig
at Smith College, on November 8, 1939[1]

Every day, for the past 88 days, I've been meditating for 20 minutes using Dan Harris's and Judson Brewer's apps. In addition to sleeping better, I've also stopped biting my fingernails. But alongside these very welcome self-improvements, new questions are emerging. Am I doing this right? Shouldn't it be easier by now? How do I know if I'm getting better? And what's the likelihood I'll make it to the end of the year? Still 50 per cent, I'd say. It's certainly not getting any easier or more pleasant. Dan told me that Buddhists describe practising meditation as like trying to tame the 'monkey mind', but for me it's more like trying to wrestle a bull elephant.

In the same way that exercising in front of a work-out video in my living room isn't as gainful as learning from a personal trainer, I'm realising that a meditation app can only take me so far. I'm in need of guidance from a real-life teacher rather than a virtual one, and I'm ready to begin my eight-week Mindfulness Based Stress Reduction (MBSR) course with Tim Goddard.

MEDITATION JOURNAL, DAY 88

Time: *45 minutes daily*

Method: *Openground, MBSR app*

Technique: *45-minute meditation led by MBSR teacher Timothea Goddard, plus mindful eating, talking and walking exercises*

Experiment notes:

I'm lying on a carpeted floor in a health centre on a stinking hot summer Sydney afternoon. My eyes are closed and I'm attempting to focus on a body scan. Right elbow … right wrist … right fingertips … The person next to me is snoring peacefully. How nice for them. Sucks for me. Left elbow … left wrist … left fingertips. Geez, 45 minutes is a long time. My back aches. Am I about to have an arthritic flare? Oh no! That would be terrible. This is not relaxing at all. I know it's not supposed to be. But still. Maybe I should have a nap too? I'm too hot to nap. I should be spending my Sunday afternoons with my kids instead of this. This is so selfish. Crikey, I'm supposed to endure this every Sunday for the next eight weeks? I should have signed up to a cooking class instead.

It's hard to believe Tim was once an anxious, overemotional young woman. She first started doing long mindfulness retreats when she was in her early 20s and now presents as an unflappable and highly regarded psychotherapist. She was one of the first MBSR teachers in Australia (there are now more than 1000 around the world) and in the last 16 years has taught more than 2000 students through Openground and trained more than 200 mindfulness teachers through the Mindfulness Training Institute – Australia and New Zealand.

The MBSR homework requires me to practise for 45 minutes a day. Despite my nicer fingernails and better sleep, despite the fact I'm a *little* more aware of my thinking patterns and mental habit loops, and despite the fact I'm getting a *little* better at noticing strong emotions without automatically reacting to them, I'm still struggling with motivation. No sooner do I direct my awareness to a point of focus (my breath, my body, or whatever else) than I find my mind thinking, planning, remembering … doing anything but what it should be doing. *Forty-five minutes*(!) of this each day … is not going to be easy.

Jon Kabat-Zinn developed MBSR in 1979 to offer hope to chronically ill people for whom conventional medicine had failed. 'Now the cracks have become Grand Canyon chasms, and everybody's suffering, including all the doctors and the medical staff and everybody in the hospitals,' he told me.

Over the decades since Jon developed MBSR, hundreds of scientists have published studies investigating if, how, why, when and for whom it works. The appeal for scientists is that it's a structured eight-week course that can be replicated; the appeal for participants is that its very title offers something most of us in this crazy-busy-overburdened world are seeking: *stress reduction.*

Before I began the course, Tim explained that many people turn to MBSR after they've tried everything else. 'People come for all sorts of reasons. A lot come because of what they'd call stress – they're not sleeping well, they're drinking too much alcohol, they're not being nice to their kids. A lot of people come because of pain and illness. People also come for anxiety and depression. Some come because they've got bipolar. Although mindfulness meditation isn't a treatment for bipolar – they would need to get special treatment for that – the very fact of having bipolar can be alienating. People also come for relationship problems more broadly.'

My MBSR group consists of mothers and fathers, professionals, performers, entrepreneurs, bakers, nurses and counsellors. There's a 19-year-old motorcycle enthusiast with striking tattoos, a mother of two young kids who is midway through her second round of breast cancer treatment, and a Catholic nun with a purple streak in her hair who's about to have major surgery for an incurable and painful autoimmune disease.

Studies show that after participating in an MBSR course, people experience better relationships[2] and stress resilience[3], relief from anxiety[4], depression[5] and chronic pain[6], and even improvement in their cancer biomarkers.[7] But after my foray into the 'Mind the Hype' issues, I wonder how an eight-week program could be beneficial for such a wide array of suffering. What's in the secret sauce?

I've committed to driving a two-hour round trip to participate in group sessions every Sunday afternoon in addition to having to meditate for 45 minutes each day. Although other mindfulness courses on offer are less intensive, Jon deliberately designed MBSR to require a big commitment from people.

'We like to joke that it's stressful to take the stress reduction program because it requires an immediate and fairly profound lifestyle change. Nobody finds the time, you *make* the time. We all have only 24 hours each day. We're always on the way to someplace else. We're always late. We're always behind. So this is a challenge, to actually *sign up* for this program. You're basically saying that you will take the time to practise whatever it is that we throw at you in the MBSR curriculum. And the formal practice is the *least* of it because the other challenges normally and naturally will spill out into the other 23 hours too.'

In addition to my daily meditation, I've also got informal mindfulness homework, including paying attention while I'm eating a meal (instead of mind*less*ly scrolling my social media feed) and having mindful conversations. In a few weeks I'll join the group for a day-long silent retreat with no distractions from all my unpleasant thoughts and feelings. (By then I'll be *fine* with seven hours of silence … right?)

It's this mix of practices in the MBSR recipe that makes it tricky for scientists trying to extract the program's key active ingredients. What causes the seemingly miraculous effects? Is it the meditation? Is it that the program forces us to slow down? Is it the gentle hatha yoga? Is it the psychotherapy delivered by a skilled and emotionally intelligent teacher like Tim? Or is it simply that, as we get to know each other in the group, we increasingly feel connected?

RELAXATION VS MINDFULNESS

Given that I've interviewed countless scientists on the subject, you would have thought that by now I'd know a thing or two about mindfulness, but I've just come across a study by neuroscientist Sara Lazar's team at Harvard University which makes me realise that I still have a lot to learn.[8]

I met Sara a few years ago when I was making *The Connection*. She's the architect of an influential meditation study which demonstrated that MBSR might beneficially change people's brains in just eight weeks and I've been periodically checking in on her research ever since.[9]

Sara's new study caught my attention because she and her team did a direct comparison of the two famous meditation programs in the US: Herbert Benson's mind-body Relaxation Response (RR) program and Jon Kabat-Zinn's MBSR program. I was aware that both of these long-running programs played a role in laying the groundwork for meditation's popularity in the West, but until now they had never been directly compared.

The study, which was published in the scientific journal *Psychosomatic Medicine*, put MBSR and the RR program head to head. Although the programs are both based on meditation, their scientific philosophies and meditative traditions have very different foundations, and subsequently the instructions and exercises taught to students are also different.

Whereas the RR program focuses on reducing stress by encouraging a physiological state of deep rest, the mindfulness program emphasises a non-judgemental attitude as its key to stress reduction. This makes sense when you consider a meditation featured in both programs called a 'body scan'. While relaxation response meditators are taught to systematically relax areas in their body, mindfulness meditators are taught to just be aware of each area, without trying to change anything.

Sara's team wondered if the nuanced differences in these techniques resulted in divergent psychological and biological signatures. And if so, what would this mean for future mind–body health recommendations?

After enlisting the support of experienced teachers and modifying the programs to match contact hours and assigned homework time, Sara's team compared the programs using subjective wellbeing measures and objective fMRI brain scans.

Eight weeks later, the results revealed both similarities and unique differences. Both groups reported a drop in perceived stress and both styles of meditation increased connectivity between brain regions associated with awareness of the physical body. But whereas the relaxation response technique activated brain regions associated with deliberate control, the mindfulness technique activated areas associated with sensory awareness and perception. The mindfulness meditators additionally reported improvements in areas such as self-compassion and rumination – two qualities that can reduce the risk of depression.

'The relaxation response program is working more through deliberate control mechanisms, while the mindfulness program is working more through sensory-awareness mechanisms. It is somewhat analogous to weight training versus aerobic exercise – both are beneficial, but each has its unique mechanism and contribution,' the study's lead author, Gunes Sevinc, a research fellow in Lazar's laboratory, told the *Harvard Gazette*.[10]

All this was revelatory for me because I'd previously thought of various mind–body practices – from yoga and tai chi, to mindfulness, relaxation and transcendental meditation – as variations of the same thing, which were all essentially aimed at stress reduction. And I'd assumed that mindfulness was about learning to relax in order to trigger a response in my body that was opposite to stress.

What I'm now understanding is that the word 'meditation' is a bit like the word 'exercise'. In the same way that swimming and running are good for me in similar and different ways, different mental training techniques have different effects.

Although emerging research is starting to further unlock some of the mechanisms of meditation, the evidence so far is unable to prescribe specific meditation techniques, in specific doses, to specific people for specific purposes.[11] For that, and for now, we'll have to rely on the guidance of experienced teachers.

Sara's study helped me to understand why I'm having so much trouble meditating. Although I knew intellectually that mindfulness was more about letting things *be* than letting them *go*, I was still trying to feel more relaxed.

The study reminded me that mindfulness isn't necessarily about relaxation at all, but rather about learning to be with whatever arises – be it pleasurable, painful, comfortable, or uncomfortable.

Stress reduction may have got me interested in mindfulness in the first place, but I'm beginning to realise that I've signed up for something that could turn out to be far more important.

The Secret Sauce

My question is now whether mindfulness meditation is the key active ingredient in MBSR. If there are other, easier and more pleasant things that I can do every day to improve my health and wellbeing, do I *really* need to do the mindful meditation practice?

Fortunately, neuroscientist Richard Davidson and his team at the Center for Healthy Minds at the University of Wisconsin-Madison did a series of clever studies investigating the same question. Richie has a reputation as a trailblazing scientist who's published hundreds of scientific papers on the neural bases of emotion and is dedicated to working out what techniques might work to promote wellbeing.

Like pretty much every scientist I've spoken to, when we met in New York Richie was careful not to oversell mindfulness. 'I think it's important that we recognise that despite the fact that there is this explosion of scientific interest, we're still at a very, *very* early stage. And sometimes lay people over-interpret and reify the findings, and have more confidence in them than we should,' he said.

In order to more rigorously put MBSR to the test, Richie and his team have developed something called the Health Enhancement Program (HEP), which is meticulously designed to be the same as MBSR in every way except for the mindfulness component.[12] HEP includes nutritional education, physical activity and music therapy. It's also delivered in a group format, by enthusiastic trainers, and there's homework, just like in MBSR.

During the all-day component of the HEP program, the participants get to attend a 'spa day' instead of sitting in silence for seven hours noticing their monkey mind. I'm half wondering if I've signed up for the wrong group.

In a HEP vs MBSR comparison study, people were randomly assigned to participate in one course or the other and filled out

MBSR		HEP	
IN-CLASS	HOMEWORK	IN-CLASS	HOMEWORK
Body Scan	Body Scan & light reading	Music Therapy: Relax, listen to music, imagery, & drawing	Relax, listen to music, imagery, & drawing
Sitting Meditation	Body Scan, Sitting Meditation, & light reading	Nutrition Education around Food Guide Pyramid	Planning meals, tracking diet, food labels, Journaling
Yoga	Alternate Yoga & Body Scan, & sitting Meditation	Functional Movement (Posture, balance, core movement)	Posture, balance, coordinated movement
Walking Meditation	Walking & other practices	Physical Activity (walk/jog. stretch)	Walking & stretching
All day (7hrs): Work with all practices, Group discussion & exercises	--	"Spa Day" (7hrs): Work with all practices, Group discussion & exercises	--

✳ MacCoon DG, Imel ZE, Rosenkranz MA, et al. The validation of an active control intervention for Mindfulness Based Stress Reduction (MBSR). Behaviour Research and Therapy. 2012, 50(1): 3–12.

questionnaires before and after. The final participant comments are fascinating:

> When I was going through the program, we were dealing with some incredible family stress, but I kept walking and it got me through a very difficult time in my life and the group did, we did some real bonding and I can't tell you how wonderful those folks were.

The program changed my life. I've lost 35 pounds since I started the program ... People notice I've lost 35 lbs and ask me how I do it. The teachers were really cool, and made you feel really comfortable.

It helped my blood pressure go down and I definitely think it helps with releasing stress. I had a lot of fun. I liked meeting once a week with the people ...

While I might have expected to read comments like these about MBSR, they were actually written by people who were assigned to the HEP group. It turned out *both* programs were rated favourably by participants. *Both* programs had similar drop-out, attendance and homework completion rates.[13] And *both* groups reported improvement in wellbeing, satisfaction with life, stress and negative emotions. (That spa day was looking better by the minute.)

More interesting was that when the researchers used a questionnaire specifically developed to measure mindfulness, they found absolutely no difference in the level of improvement from MBSR or HEP.[14] In other words, regardless of whether people did a program that included formal meditation, they reported feeling better and more mindful afterwards.

I asked Tim Goddard about this and she thought that those in the HEP program were actually getting inadvertent mindful awareness training through the music therapy, imagery and drawing components of the program. Craig Hassed from Monash University also warned me against a sweeping conclusion that MBSR was no better than placebo because researchers don't yet have a good placebo for mindfulness studies. Sugar pills used in gold-standard trials for new pharmaceutical treatments are known as *inactive* placebos, whereas the HEP lifestyle program is known as an *active* placebo. He suspects that using the same methodology as drug trials may not be the most effective way of studying mindfulness. 'As Mark Twain said, "Studying humour is like dissecting a frog. You may know a lot, but you wind up with a dead frog". If researchers don't take the difficulties into account there is a distinct danger of killing the frog rather than understanding it.'

To me, this speaks volumes about the difficulty of doing research on mindfulness. Nevertheless, the results from the HEP vs MBSR studies are crucial for the future of meditation research because they underscore what we all already know to be true – that *any* health program, provided that it is rigorous, medically sound, credible and delivered by experts, will probably be good for you, regardless of whether or not there's a component of formal mindfulness.

I suspect the reason why programs like MBSR have taken off is because there are few similar programs on offer within our mainstream medical system, which relies on either surgical or pharmacological treatment methods (and is largely driven by profit and loss rather than health and wellbeing).

THE ART OF READING A SCIENTIFIC PAPER

Whether it's *Current Directions in Psychological Science* or *The Lancet Commission on Global Mental Health and Sustainable Development*, there are few things in the world that make me feel quite so intellectually inept as attempting to read a scientific journal.

It's not the scientists' fault that their articles consist of 95-word sentences and jargonistic gobbledegook. After all, the peer-review process means that the aim of their game is not to write for popular consumption but, rather, to impress a handful of specialists working in their sub-sub-discipline.

Nevertheless, in a world full of fake news and brand-funded health advertorials, I want to be able to make well-informed decisions and implement healthy lifestyle changes based on accurate, balanced and complete information. This has necessitated mastering the art of reading a scientific paper.

My 10-step process goes something like this:

1. Intrigue

I'm looking for a solution for a health-related issue. Let's say it's my insomnia. And I'm curious to know what the latest research shows on, say, mindfulness and insomnia. 'This can't be too hard,' I tell myself. 'After all, I like reading.'

2. Derailment

The study I want to read is trapped behind an online paywall: $34.95 for a 1200-word article! At an average of three to four mindfulness-related scientific papers a day, I'll be flat broke by the end of this project.

3. Resourcefulness

I remember that my State Library membership gives me free online access to most health journals. In two clicks of my mouse I'm logged in and have the full article displayed on my screen. I'm in business.

4. Preparedness
I clear my sit-stand desk until it's a Zen-like temple of journalistic productivity. My digital highlighter and electronic notation tools are open and all foreseeable distractions are eliminated: schedule clear, notifications off, phone on silent, email and web browser closed. It's time to soak up some cutting-edge knowledge.

5. Optimism
I begin with the paper's abstract, a four- or five-sentence summary which tells me what to expect. I forgive the long sentences (after all, they're scientists not, ahem, award-winning journalists), gloss over a few befuddling acronyms, and generally get the gist that:
1. Scientists are interested in the link between mindfulness and insomnia.
2. They did a study which showed mindfulness helped insomnia; but
3. They don't know exactly why and more research is needed.

This is a cinch, I think. *I'm on fire. I should totally be a scientist.*

6. Doubt
Full of confident gusto, I embark on reading the experiment's background, methodology, results and final discussion. Words such as 'soteriological' and 'metacognition' mingle with acronyms such as 'MBI' and 'OA' and I'm vaguely aware that

the entire afternoon has passed and I still haven't read the
second paragraph.

7. Diversion

There are suddenly many, *many* things infinitely more
important than finding out about the latest science on
mindfulness and insomnia. What's the time? What should I
make for dinner? What's a healthy version of ice-cream I can
make for my kids' dessert tonight? Watermelon. Even better,
frozen watermelon. I should go freeze some watermelon. Oh
darn, now I have that children's song by Justine Clarke stuck
in my head. Quick, think of something else or the watermelon
song will be stuck in my head when I try to meditate later.
Now the chorus of 'Let it Go' from *Frozen* pops into my
head … Oh no! That's even *worse*. Change track. Have animals
been to space yet? If so, what was the first animal to go into
space?

8. Abandonment

I abandon my endeavours to understand the latest research on
mindfulness and insomnia. I go to bed. I have insomnia. When
sleep finally arrives, a talking snowman haunts my dreams.

9. Resolution

Bleary eyed and despairing, the next day I try again. I forbid
myself to read the next sentence without understanding each
and every complicated word and acronym in the current one.
The sentences start making sense. It's taken four hours to read
a four-page paper, but I actually get it. And it's *really* helpful. It

turns out that mindfulness training may help insomnia by both calming my body's biological system and also giving me an ability to become aware of my own mental state, allowing me to then change my relationship to it.

10. Self-righteousness

I now know stuff. *Scientific* stuff. *Useful* scientific stuff. I should tell other people about it. I should write this up in a blog. Oh crap. That means I have to make this all make sense to others ... The cow that jumped over the moon. That was the first animal in space. Thank you, four-year-old Theodore Harvey, your mother thinks you're a comic genius.

Immeasurably Better

In my struggle to reconcile that science is full of shades of grey instead of the black and white answers I prefer, I got back in touch with Nicholas Van Dam, the lead author of the 'Mind the Hype' paper from Melbourne University.

'That's a hard one, I don't know,' he said. 'Our default as scientists if we want to know whether or not mindfulness works is to hook the person that's doing the meditation up to every possible thing we can think of. Let's get blood, let's get cortisol samples, let's get saliva, let's look at their brain, let's look at their heart, their respiration ... Let's come up with every possible thing we can. And it may be that the effects on the person are on the person as a whole and that you may best observe those effects in that person's life. Some of the most interesting studies to me have not looked directly at the person who's doing the practice.'

Nicholas pointed me to an unorthodox study where therapists in training were randomised in groups to either get Zen meditation practice or relaxation training.[15] (Zen is a form of Buddhist meditation which involves mindfulness training.) When the researchers looked at the outcomes of the therapist's clients they found that the clients of the therapists who received Zen training got better faster and stayed better longer. 'So we really need to think carefully about where we are looking for the effects. If this is working, where would we observe it? And it might not necessarily always be biology, particularly not in the short term. It takes a while for us to change physiology.'

Another unconventional study combed through the health records of over 18 000 people who were considered to be 'high-utilisers' of healthcare services and found that if people had done a Mindfulness Based Cognitive Therapy (MBCT) course they used fewer healthcare services, including needing to see a psychiatrist less frequently.[16] Although the researchers hypothesised that people went to the doctor less because they had better moods and less anxiety, they couldn't say if it was the mindfulness training that did it or just the fact that they'd been given group support and psycho-education.

To me, this highlights a key point. As well as my own insights during MBSR, I'm starting to witness some of my new MBSR friends feeling better, but I don't think I'm getting closer to drawing out what the key change agents are: whether it's the skilled instruction and wisdom of Tim, whether it's the power of social support, whether it's the effect that the program is having on our relationships or attitude to our lives. Or maybe, just maybe it truly is as simple as sitting for 45 minutes a day practising mindfulness.

I went into MBSR with my usual journalistic drive, wanting to work out what 'it' is that results in all the compelling scientific data. I wanted to get to the bottom of things. But just like any good recipe, it's when the ingredients combine in the pot and simmer away for eight weeks that we discover the real secret in the sauce.

There is one intriguing finding from the MBSR vs HEP studies done by Richie Davidson and his team that seems worth investigating. Although both programs are effective at reducing anxiety, distress, hostility and attentional stability, people who are taught MBSR show a reduction in inflammation following social stress, and better tolerance of pain.[17,18] Given this – and the fact we're in the midst of an opioid addiction epidemic on top of all the other mental health problems – an evidence-backed, non-pharmacological solution to pain is no small thing.[19–23]

CHAPTER FIVE

Discomfortable

Autobiography in Five Short Chapters

Chapter One

I walk down the street.

There is a deep hole in the sidewalk.

I fall in.

I am lost … I am helpless.

It isn't my fault.

It takes forever to find a way out.

Chapter Two

I walk down the same street.

There is a deep hole in the sidewalk.

I pretend I don't see it.

I fall in again.

I can't believe I am in the same place. But it isn't my fault.

It still takes a long time to get out.

Chapter Three

I walk down the same street.

There is a deep hole in the sidewalk.

I see it is there.

I still fall in … it's a habit.

My eyes are open.

I know where I am.

It is my fault … I get out immediately.

Chapter Four

I walk down the same street.

There is a deep hole in the sidewalk.

I walk around it.

Chapter Five

I walk down another street.

– by Portia Nelson[1]

Knowing Better

Judson Brewer from Brown University defines the word 'addiction' as 'continued use, despite adverse consequences'.[2] In other words, you're addicted to something if you keep doing it despite the fact that it's bad for you. If he's right I may be in trouble, because it means that, among other things, I'm addicted to … filmmaking.

Ever since my husband, Jules, and I decided to make another documentary life has been full on. Despite the movie industry's glamorous reputation, the reality is far from that.

As independent filmmakers, we finance the majority of the production ourselves, which means we have to work full time to pay for the full-time work of making the film. Throw two full-time young kids into the mix and *ta-da* ... mayhem. While the kids are thankfully none the wiser to my second workday that kicks off post-story time, the result for me is a flare-up of my illness.

Despite being a health journalist and despite knowing better, I have fallen into the hole in my own metaphorical sidewalk and have been putting work before health. I've been dropping crucial hours of sleep in order to get film grant applications completed before deadline and I've been spending way too many days hunched over my computer, researching and lining up interviews, without exercising regularly in the way that I know I must in order to be well.

The arthritic pain is similar to what it feels like after throwing myself into a new exercise program with too much gusto, only I haven't been to the gym or a yoga class in weeks, nor is the pain improving after a day or two. I'm stiff and sore, my fingers are tender, my neck is rigid and the joints in my hips and lower back are inflamed. Even the connective tissues in my arms and legs are painful to touch. Although I don't have the immobilising chronic fatigue I once had, in the last two weeks my pain levels have skyrocketed from a zero to a seven out of 10. The irony that the very documentary experiment that is destabilising my work–life balance is all about trying to find health and wellbeing through mindfulness is not lost on me.

I'm now in the final week of Mindfulness Based Stress Reduction (MBSR). Part of me secretly hoped that all I needed to do was meditate every day and my illness would be magically cured. But this arthritic flare-up confirms everything that the last six years of my research have uncovered: good health is not achieved by focusing on one ingredient but is dependent on taking care of myself as a whole – mind, body, soul, and everything in between.

I'm not the only one who's optimistically turned to MBSR in the hope of discovering a cure for chronic illness and pain. Among our group of 15, two are in the midst of breast cancer treatment, another suffers debilitating migraines, one woman has unrelenting pelvic pain from an ineffective surgery, while another has searing nerve pain in her jaw from a dental treatment gone wrong.

Then there's Mary-Lynne Cochrane, a Catholic nun whose crippling arthritis has eaten away at the soft tissues in her body, causing bone-on-bone complications and resulting in 23 major surgeries to replace her joints. Mary-Lynne joined our MBSR group because she has not only recently quit her opioid pain medication (to which she was addicted – yes, a drug-addicted nun), she's also been advised to come off her anti-inflammatory medication in order to prepare for her 24th surgery. 'It's been an up- and downhill battle and I want to develop more to be able to control it when I have a flare-up without having to go back onto the medication. There will be times when I'll have to take it, but I want to be able to live the rest of my life that I have left being healthy and training my own brain to help me,' she told the group.

The daunting thing about our not-so-merry band is that we're representative of the worldwide chronic pain predicament. According to a paper recently published by the US National Academies of Sciences, Engineering and Medicine, 11.2 per cent of the American adult population (that's 25.3 *million* people) are in chronic pain. In the next 12 months, 100 million people will suffer.[3,4] This comes at a cost of approximately $635 billion a year to the US economy – more than the costs of cancer and heart disease treatment combined.[5]

It's a similar situation elsewhere in the world. In the UK, the *British Medical Journal* reports that some 28 million adults live with pain that has lasted three months or more, while in Europe and Australia the ratio is one in five.[6,7]

I know all too well that behind these statistics lies a heavy emotional burden and that spending every conscious moment in pain is unbearable. It's not just the pain that hurts. In a cruel cycle, pain also disrupts my mood, sleep, work and social life, which also zaps my motivation to exercise and eat well.[8]

It's little wonder that up to 85 per cent of those in chronic pain are also affected by severe depression. Ten per cent of people who commit suicide also have chronic pain.[9–11]

Surely we could be doing better? One person who thinks so is Vidyamala Burch, a mindfulness teacher who's normally based in the UK. Vidyamala runs a charitable organisation called Breathworks that offers online and in-person chronic pain programs that are in part inspired by Jon Kabat-Zinn's MBSR. She happened to be teaching in Sydney and we met up for lunch on a glorious autumnal April day.

CASE STUDY #2 – PART 1

Vidyamala Burch – Founder, Breathworks
[Edited transcript]

Me: Can you give me a description of what it is like to be in your body?

Vidyamala: A doctor would describe my medical diagnosis today as having incomplete paraplegia, paralysed bowel, paralysed bladder, and having chronic neuropathic and muscular skeletal pain. So my lived experience of being in this body today is that I've got pain, all the time.

Me: How did it come to this?

Vidyamala: I was brought up in New Zealand, a very beautiful, free, active childhood. I was very sporty. Then when I was 16, I was doing lifesaving practice and I lifted someone out of the swimming pool. And it turned out that I had a condition called spondylolisthesis and that my vertebrae had fractured.

At the beginning of my 17th year, in 1977, I had a spinal fusion operation to bolt my spine together but unfortunately there were complications. Six months later I had part of my vertebrae removed. So I went from being this really sporty, athletic, outdoorsy girl to being someone who was living with chronic pain. I lost a whole year of school.

In 1983 when I was 23, I was in a car and the driver fell asleep at the wheel and we ploughed into a telegraph pole. I had all the damage in my lower spine and now I had a fracture in the middle of my spine. But I tried to keep living a normal life. I was able to convince myself that there's not really anything wrong with me and I could just be like everybody else.

I kept working but eventually I collapsed. I ended up in a neurosurgical intensive care ward. The medical team made it clear to me there was no medical, magical cure. My spine was very, very damaged. More surgery wasn't going to help. I needed to learn to live with it, somehow.

I had a dark night of the soul where I honestly thought I was going to go mad. I had part of my mind saying, 'I can't bear this, I'm going to go crazy, I cannot get through till the morning,' and another part of my mind saying, 'But you have to.' It was like someone was turning these screws inside my head. My body was hurting, but it was a mental torture and I was getting more and more desperate.

Then at a certain point, another voice came in and said very, very clearly, 'You just have to live this moment.' The message was, forget about the morning, just be present now and now and now and now, and then the morning will arrive. And my experience changed from being in a vice, to one of greater ease.

That was in 1985. I was 25 years old. Now I'm 58 and I still feel that that has been the most profound moment of my life and everything that's followed since then, all the meditation, becoming a Buddhist, founding Breathworks, is still trying to make sense of that.

What You Don't Think, Won't Hurt

The Blessed One said, 'When touched with a feeling of pain, the
uninstructed run-of-the-mill person sorrows, grieves, & laments, beats
his breast, becomes distraught. So he feels two pains, physical & mental.
Just as if they were to shoot a man with an arrow and, right afterward,
were to shoot him with another one, so that he would feel the pains of
two arrows; in the same way, when touched with a feeling of pain, the
uninstructed run-of-the-mill person sorrows, grieves, & laments, beats
his breast, becomes distraught. So he feels two pains, physical & mental.'

Sallatha Sutta: The Arrow, translated from the
Pāli by Thanissaro Bhikkhu[12]

When I consider it from an evolutionary perspective, acute pain makes sense. The throb of a sprained ankle, the ache of an infected tooth, the stab of a rogue Lego piece underfoot – these painful experiences all tell me when things are dangerous, when I'm sick, and when I need to take it easy in order to recover. In fact, people with a genetic mutation that causes them to feel no pain have been known to lose hearing because of untreated ear infections, burn themselves on hot surfaces, and develop deformities from continuing to use unfelt broken limbs.[13–15]

Although helpful, acute pain is far from pleasant, and for the majority of us who are able to feel it, modern medicine offers effective remedies in the form of medication, injections, and bandaids administered by loving mothers.

As for chronic pain, the kind that starts one ordinary Wednesday morning and is still there 10 years later, we actually know very little and the grim reality is that there are currently no medical treatments that work well.

Despite the evidence that anti-inflammatory drugs can cause severe side effects and that opioids are highly addictive, in the absence of alternatives these medications are still widely prescribed.[16] According to a report by the US Surgeon General, 91 Americans die from pain medication overdoses every day.[17–20] Although this is driven primarily by illegal, not medical, abuse of prescription pills, a study of over 135000 opioid overdose victims found that 13 per cent were chronic pain patients.[21] In England, more than half a million people have been prescribed opioids continuously for three years or more, putting them at risk of addiction.[22]

The problem with thinking that a single pill, injection or surgical procedure will resolve chronic pain is that it ignores what the evidence shows: that the brain and biological signature of the helpful, precautionary (or 'good') kind of pain is uniquely different from the ongoing, chronic (or 'bad') kind of pain. Chronic pain physiologically rewires us over time and involves complex neurological, biological and psychological factors.[23] Chronic pain is as much about the physical sensation as it is about the cognitive and emotional response to it. Far from being 'all in the mind', neuroscientists are actually calling for chronic pain to be classified as a disease in its own right.[24,25]

The much-needed next step here is developing, testing and verifying approaches to chronic pain which recognise its multidimensional complexity; approaches which, as Jon Kabat-Zinn told me, could catch people falling through 'the chasms' of a reductionist medical system which often treats us as little more than a set of test results from which to write prescriptions.

MEDITATION JOURNAL, DAY 121

Time: *45 minutes daily*
Method: *Openground, MBSR app*
Technique: *45-minute meditation led by MBSR teacher Tim Goddard, plus mindful eating, talking and walking exercises*

Experiment notes:
I'm in my car, meditating before I go into the house to face witching hour at home. I've been in such a funk today. The kids both woke up multiple times last night. Terrible sleep = terrible mood = terrible meditation experience. Note to self, meditating while hungry is awful. Every thought that enters my mind is tinged with an unpleasant edge. Hungry. Angry. Hangry. My back is aching. My neck is stiff. Too much sitting, not enough yoga. Pain. Pain. Pain. Monumentally unpleasant. Is this what my whole life will be like? Always in pain? What if my illness gets worse? What if it starts attacking my organs? How can I be a good mother if I end up in a wheelchair? I notice my thoughts. I notice their tone. Huh. So dramatic. The intensity falls away. The pain is different now. It doesn't seem so bad. Has it changed? Or has my attitude to it changed? I get curious. Huh. Interesting. What does the pain feel like? Where exactly is it in my body? There, in my neck. But where in my neck? I can't find the exact place. Isn't it interesting what happens when I turn towards the pain instead of resisting it? Is equanimity the right word? Bravery perhaps?

Stories from frontline pain clinics report that when patients are asked to rate their pain on a scale of one to 10, with 10 being akin to torture, many rate their pain at 12.[26] I can relate. Pain which persists for months, years or a lifetime goes hand in glove with catastrophic feelings of distress.

And so enters mindfulness training, which sits comfortably alongside conventional care, can be delivered in supportive groups, along with pain education, and can also be practised at home.[27]

In 1985, Jon Kabat-Zinn and his colleagues demonstrated that chronic pain patients reported improvements in pain symptomology and quality of life after completing his MBSR program and that the improvements were sustained three years later.[28,29] Jon's study was the spark and although recent meta-analyses are careful not to oversell how much we know, a number of high-quality trials have now linked mindfulness-based interventions with reduced pain, reduced symptoms of depression, and improved quality of life compared with treatment as usual (such as support groups, education, stress management, and waitlist controls).[30,31] As a result, some of the biggest champions of mindfulness are no longer Buddhist monks but doctors wanting to offer adjunct solutions.

I'm intrigued why mindfulness is catching on among medical professionals, so I called my friend and mentor Craig Hassed. Since we met in 2012 I've lost count of the number of experts I've interviewed, but Craig's encyclopaedic knowledge of the scientific literature showing how our mind impacts our health and vice versa is second to none. Craig is the recipient of the Medal of the Order of Australia (OAM) and is renowned for embedding mindfulness in mainstream medical education and throughout other faculties at Monash University.

Jules (who has the handy skills of being able to both produce *and* film documentaries) and I flew to Melbourne and sat down to pick Craig's brain about why mindfulness is gaining momentum in mainstream medical treatment of chronic pain.

'With pain, acute or chronic, but especially chronic, we experience the sensation followed by the mental and emotional reaction to the sensation,' Craig told me. 'An old metaphor that's used is that it's like two arrows. The first arrow is like the experience of something uncomfortable. But the second arrow that really harms us more is when we ruminate or worry over the pain, get angry about it, or feel afraid of it.'

He explained that mindfulness teaches me to gently notice my pain without being emotionally reactive to it, and this enables me to avoid amplifying the experience by getting caught up in a catastrophic internal monologue: *Why me? When will this stop? How am I going to be there for the kids if I'm always sick?*

'Pain becomes just a sensation and that makes it easier to gently unhook your attention and to re-engage with what's going on around you – the food you're eating, the people you're with, the work you're doing.'

Craig then gave me a number of intriguing brain studies that hint at possible neurological underpinnings of the 'second arrow' analogy. Sara Lazar's team at Harvard have demonstrated that when experienced meditators, who had an average of 5979 meditation hours under their belt, were given an experimental electrical pulse that felt like a sharp needle prick, there was a 'decoupling' between sensory and appraisal-related brain networks.[32] Similar findings have been recorded both in experienced Zen practitioners as well as inexperienced meditators who have only practised for a few days.[33] But as far as I can tell, studies have so far only examined the effects of mindfulness training with regard to acute pain.

In the absence of studies on people using mindfulness for chronic pain, the first-hand accounts are my most valuable resource. In our final week of MBSR, Mary-Lynne, the Catholic nun, reported feeling more comfortable than ever before. 'I've been on morphine all week because I'm in so much pain,' she told the group. 'But I'm not agitated by it. When I do my body scan meditation, it's like the pain is there, but I can bring my awareness to other parts of my body that aren't sore. I can see that there's a whole to everything. A whole to the pain. My body scan is changing my thinking and has made a huge difference in the last eight weeks.'

CASE STUDY #2 – PART 2

Vidyamala Burch – Founder, Breathworks
[Edited transcript]

Vidyamala: I came across the work of Jon Kabat-Zinn and his book *Full Catastrophe Living* and what he talked about was turning towards your direct experience, turning towards your pain, investigating your pain, getting to know your pain, rather than trying to escape your pain.

What I'd tried in the past was a kind of escapist meditation to try to generate a different experience from the one that I was having and sometimes I even felt really happy, but it was a kind of false happiness, trying to occupy a fantasy world and there was a lot of strain involved. So I thought, oh my God, that's the missing link. I haven't learned how to turn *towards* my direct experience. So that became my mission.

I started meditating for an hour a day and also practising mindfulness in all aspects of my life. I learned about pacing – about timing myself, not pushing myself. And it really changed my life enormously. I have a very effective life now. I travel globally. I teach globally. I've still got chronic pain. I'm still disabled. I've still got a paralysed bowel and bladder, my legs don't work properly, but I have a *really* good life.

My story isn't one of a miracle cure. It's a story of healing, rather than cure. And I think this is very, very important because for many years I felt I was a failure – I can't manage to earn a living, I can't manage to sort my life out, and I can't cure my pain – but there's a distinction between healing and cure, and the real healing is where you learn to live with your life as it is with grace, with dignity, with acceptance, with courage, with kindness.

Mindfulness isn't going to unfuse my spine. It's not. It's not going to heal my nervous system. But mindfulness has enabled me to profoundly heal my response to life as it is and for me, that's a much greater miracle because we've all got bodies that will age, we've all got bodies that things will go wrong, and if the paradigm is you're only succeeding if you can have a perfect body at all times, through all stages of life, we're all going to fail.

> I'm not actually very interested in cure. I'm interested in learning to live with my life, whatever arrives in any day. We can't control what arrives in our life, but we can control how we respond to it.

Don't Take it Personally

When Vidyamala was younger, she would never have chosen to become an expert in suffering, or to lead a life of teaching others how to suffer, but I found our encounter in Sydney nothing short of remarkable. Her enthusiasm for life, her clarity of mind and bright-eyed joy, despite how much pain I knew she was experiencing, were palpable. If I kept up this mindfulness training, would I feel this way too? One thing I do know is that the discipline of sitting for 45 minutes a day is teaching me how to sit with my physical discomfort without becoming emotionally reactive and worrying that my health is in tatters.

It's not just my physical pain that I'm getting better at facing. I'm also 'leaning in' to my difficult thoughts and feelings instead of doing everything I can to avoid or distract myself from them. My relationships with people that have been the source of so much of my emotional pain and heartache are also shifting – I'm learning how to anchor myself in the storm without getting tossed around.

The surprising truth is that in becoming at ease with my 'dis-ease' I'm not actually feeling any happier. It's more like I'm becoming more accepting of my *unhappiness*. I'm learning *how* to suffer; how to sit with physical and emotional pain, with unpleasant and uncomfortable experiences, and know that things will probably be okay. I'm learning how to notice that I'm in a blue mood and not force an improvement via a new shopping purchase, or a social media binge; and how to deal with uncertainty, disappointment, loss, and (shock, horror) … *failure*.

I'm learning to be okay with all this and to notice the ever-changing nature of all that is both bad and good in my life. I'm more comfortable with the discomfort that is part and parcel of being human. This is what I'm calling being more … *discomfortable*.

The fact that daily meditation isn't making me happier may be controversial for meditation devotees, or to anyone who's

read the titles of some bestselling meditation books (*The Art of Happiness, Real Happiness, The Book of Joy* ... to name a few). Even Dan Harris – a fellow critical-thinking journalist – talks about how meditation makes him '10 per cent' happier.

I also realise that as far as the self-help industry goes, it's easier to sell the promise of peace, love and happiness than 'Learning to be Comfortable with the Inescapable Suffering of Life'. But in my view there's an important distinction between becoming happier and learning the *how* of being unhappy.

I was raised in a culture that reveres triumph over adversity, flawlessness, the promise of miracles, and happy endings. In this oversimplified, Disney-fied version of life, Cinderella doesn't end up scrubbing floors to earn her living, nor does Snow White develop an incurable chronic illness after eating the poison apple, and as for the impoverished Charlie Bucket who's eaten nothing but cabbage soup his whole life? He wins a golden ticket and inherits a chocolate empire.

My mythological diet of happily-ever-afters has meant that whenever bad things have happened in my life I've railed against them as if they were wrong, or unfair, or 'not meant to be'. In fact, I've invested 37 years in employing unconscious, often elaborate mental and behavioural strategies in a fruitless attempt to avoid uncomfortable emotions and pain.

According to Tim, I'm not the first person to come to this realisation during MBSR. 'There's an assumption that when suffering comes along, it's an aberration. It shouldn't be happening to *me*. Someone has a bad accident or a hideous disease comes their way, it's like, we really don't expect these things to happen to me, me, *me*. And so there's something about mindfulness meditation, which trains us to go, "Okay, there are lots of unpleasant things arising, it's not personal." It's a skilful way to meet that suffering and not spend a lot of energy in reactivity. What people find often is that it shifts and changes it.'

All this can be summed up by a phrase often used by mindfulness teachers: *Life sucks. Everything changes. Don't take it personally.* Although, Tim also rightly pointed out that life doesn't *always* suck and that good things do, and often do, happen too. She amends the expression to say, 'Life sucks *and* sings. Everything changes. Don't take it personally.'

What's the likelihood that I will make it to day 365? 60 per cent.

CHAPTER SIX

Waking Up

MEDITATION JOURNAL, DAY 171

Time: *45 minutes daily*
Method: *Self-guided meditation*
Technique: *Mental noting*

Experiment notes:
I'm on a plane on my way home from Melbourne. I'm practising
'mental noting', itemising whatever is happening in my
experience. I start by directing my attention to my breath at my
nostrils. I note, breath in. Breath out. Chest. Rising. Falling.
White noise. Rising. Falling. I feel the pull of work thinking. I
note, work thinking. Rising. Falling. Nothing to do. Nowhere
to be. Just here. Just now. Rising. Falling. There is a sense of my
body. I note, body. There is a rattle of a food cart. I note, rattle.
There is a presence of the person next to me. I note, other.
Rising. Falling. I think of home. Rising. Falling. I think about
my kids. Rising. Falling. I feel a smile. Rising. Falling. There is
love. There is joy. There is contentment. My awareness rests in

---

the feeling of contentment. Content. Content. Content. Gee, this is really nice. Is this the 'it'? Is this what I've been aiming for in all my practice? Maybe the monk Matthieu Ricard feels like this all the time. Maybe that's why he's the happiest man alive. I want more. Oh wait, 'it' is gone. I am thinking. Breath in. Breath out. Chest. Rising. Falling.

This morning I woke at 5.45 a.m. to meditate.

I can't believe I just wrote that. As a natural-born night owl, this is no small thing. Although I'm not bouncing out of bed every morning (my genetic programming means I'll *never* be a true lark), the fact that I'm beginning to even *want* to meditate at that ludicrous hour a couple of days a week is unexpected. I even own a meditation stool now. I wonder if this officially makes me 'a meditator'?

It's not getting any easier, though. After more than 100 hours of practice, 14 expert interviews, two in-depth case studies – and after witnessing the profound effects that MBSR had on some of my fellow MBSR groupies – practising mindfulness every day is still hard work. But I *am* starting to feel that it's worth it.

Since increasing my practice to 45 minutes a day, I've noticed a kind of 'dose effect': a difference in mental clarity. My mind feels like it did when I was younger. Thinking is clearer, more easeful, as though by setting aside 45 minutes of solitude each day – time where my mind is free from any other stimulation other than what is already there – and by continually practising just letting my mental experiences *be*, there's a kind of inner processing that occurs. It's as if I'm de-fragging my mental hard drive, or allowing all the mud in my mental bucket to settle to the bottom, leaving clearer thinking behind.

I can't find any scientific literature to explain the 'mud-in-the-bucket' settling effects I'm experiencing. The closest thing I've found is research done on mice which demonstrated that their brains have a glymphatic system which clears protein build-up during sleep.[1,2] Although this is interesting, equating the mind-clarifying effects of meditation that I'm experiencing with the brain-garbage-disposal system that happens in the minds of sleeping mice is a bit of a stretch.

There is some interesting work emerging on something called the brain's Default Mode Network (DMN), which I've made a note to look into, but I'm also surprised that few studies look into the dose question of mindfulness training. Is there an optimal amount of practice I should be doing?

Scientists think that the more experienced the meditator, the bigger the change in brain structure, but this is not universally true.[3] Some studies show 30 minutes of meditation per day for eight weeks can increase the density of grey matter in brain regions associated with memory, stress, and empathy, while others show that only 20 minutes per day for four days improves cognitive skills and decreases pain sensitivity.[4–6] But there are also other studies that do not show any dose effects whatsoever.

As is often the case, the research is mixed. I'm going to have to get more comfortable with the fact that there might not be neat scientific correlates to explain all the first-hand experiences that I'm documenting in this experiment.

Ancient Brain, Smart Phone

The more easeful, almost childhood-like mental clarity has made me aware of how overloaded I was, even just a few weeks ago. I feel a bit like Neo in *The Matrix* after he's just woken up: I can suddenly see all the forces around me competing for my attention. I keep having these moments of awakening – realising that I'm lost in an online news story that I never intended to read, or mindlessly scrolling a bottomless feed of highlights from other people's social media lives.

With my newly developing skill of being *discomfortable* – more comfortable with my discomfort – I can see that I'm using my smartphone as a kind of emotional pick-me-up. I wake up in the morning, not quite ready to face the day, and check my phone. A moment of boredom in an elevator? Check my phone. Feeling a bit miffed after someone criticised me? Check my phone. Kids being difficult? Check my phone. Having trouble constructing a sentence for this book chapter? Check my phone ... *Aw. The update from the kids' daycare centre tells me that Theo is working on a building project at the moment and Izzy is covered in paint. So cute. I wonder if anyone has sent me an email reply about that grant application yet? No. How disappointing. What about the news headlines? I wonder if anything interesting is happening in the world* ... And there went 20 minutes of valuable time I'd allocated for writing today.

Like the pull of a rip-tide, whenever I'm experiencing a slightly unpleasant moment of transition in my day, I want ... no, *need* to reach for my phone. I'm not alone. One study found the average smartphone user checks for updates

85 times a day. In a normal waking day, that's about once every 11 minutes.[7]

I wonder how much of my digital diet is really just junk: empty mental calories that seem tasty at the time but might actually be doing more harm than good. Have I been missing golden opportunities to get meaningful work done, or rare moments of valuable reflection, or precious chances to savour the very essence of what makes a good life ... because I've been mindlessly buried in my smartphone?

Given smartphones are relatively new, the scientific field studying their impact on our health is still emerging, but already there's alarming evidence of lost productivity[8], lost brain function[9], lost wellbeing[10], lost work–life balance[11], lost sleep[12], lost human connection[13], and even lost lives[14] resulting from inappropriate use.

After recently catching myself wanting to check my email instead of enjoying a fleeting moment of Saturday morning cuddles in bed with my kids, I asked Judson Brewer why these devices are so darn captivating. Among other things, Jud investigates the brain basis of habit and addiction, and whether mindfulness can help people overcome them. He explained that the same brain circuits that make me seek out all the things that are necessary to ensure my survival – such as food, comfort, heat and love – are also triggered when I use the apps on my phone. 'We have these ancient brains that haven't quite evolved as quickly as our cellphones.'

Because of something called 'operant conditioning' (or 'reinforcement learning') – a brain-based learning system that we share with sea slugs and all other animals – our behaviour is largely driven by learning to do things that result in positive outcomes, and learning not do things that result in negative outcomes.[15,16] This is how we form habits – both good and bad. It turns out that many smartphone apps hijack this cue-behaviour-reward system.

Let's say I'm going about my day and have a witty insight that I think others might enjoy. This would be a 'cue'. When I then use my smartphone to share the insight on social media, I perform a 'behaviour'. And when I get likes, comments and retweets, I receive my 'reward'. The more I do this, the more my behaviour is reinforced, and before I know it I've developed an automated habit: a habit that can be so compelling that despite having a perfectly delightful time with my kids, I can feel the need for a quick positive neurochemical hit by checking my Twitter feed.

Jud spent his early career treating people with drug dependencies. While many of us tend to think of addiction as something that only relates to smokers, heavy drinkers, or people with chemical drug reliance, addiction is really the extreme end of reward-based learning behaviour. Jud reminded me of his definition of addiction: 'continued use despite adverse consequences'.[17] In other words, you're addicted to something if you keep doing it despite the fact that it's bad for you.

Before now, I've never really valued my attention. But I'm realising that my attention is the *everything* through which I experience the world. And now that I can see things more clearly, I'm starting to wonder what I've been mindlessly missing. Perhaps, more importantly, what – or *who* – has been missing me?

STRAIGHT FROM THE HORSE'S MOUTH ...

Excerpt from 2017 article in *The Guardian* featuring Sean Parker, Facebook's founding president:

> When Facebook was being developed the objective was: 'How do we consume as much of your time and conscious attention as possible? ... It's a social-validation feedback loop ... exactly the kind of thing that a hacker like myself would come up with, because you're exploiting a vulnerability in human psychology.'[18]

*

Excerpt from 2017 article in *The Guardian* featuring Justin Rosenstein, the Facebook engineer who created the 'like' button:

> Rosenstein had tweaked his laptop's operating system to block Reddit, banned himself from Snapchat, which he compares to heroin, and imposed limits on his use of Facebook. But even that wasn't enough. In August, the 34-year-old tech executive took a more radical step to restrict his use of social media and other addictive technologies. Rosenstein purchased a new iPhone and instructed his assistant to set up a parental-control feature to prevent him from downloading any apps.[19]

*

Excerpt from 2018 article in *Business Insider* featuring Evan Williams, co-founder of Twitter and founder of Medium:

> Today, Williams has all but given up on social media, he tells *Business Insider*. 'I've pretty much weaned myself off of being addicted to social media for instance, which I was at one time,' he says. That's an astonishing thing for the founder, former CEO, and current board member of Twitter to say. It is akin to Mark Zuckerberg announcing that he tries to not spend time on Facebook.[20]

*

Excerpt from 2017 article in *Thrive Global*, reporting on comments made by Tony Fadell, designer of the first iPhone:

> 'I worry what my grandkids are going to think,' he said to Anderson Cooper. 'Will it be "He's the guy that destroyed society?"'[21]

*

Excerpt from 2014 article in the *New York Times* about the late Apple CEO and founder Steve Jobs:

> 'So, your kids must love the iPad?' I asked Mr Jobs … The company's first tablet was just hitting the shelves. 'They haven't used it,' he told me. 'We limit how much technology our kids use at home.'[22]

Totally Addicted

Hello, my name is Shannon and I think I might be addicted to my smartphone.

Whether or not being a 'constant checker' constitutes having a full-blown addiction is currently the subject of academic debate, partly because researchers are still working out a universally accepted definition of smartphone addiction, but one thing I know for sure is that there are a thousand more pleasurable and meaningful ways to start my day than looking at my phone.[23]

While some experts go as far as to liken screen time to 'digital heroin'[24], and *Wired Magazine* (which is guided in large part by a belief in technology's capacity to deliver humanity from ruin)

has started running articles with titles such as 'It's Time for A Serious Talk About the Science of Tech Addiction'[25], sociologists respond by saying such doomsaying is overblown and that just as when the printing press was bemoaned as the end of humanity, so too is the 'moral panic' about our smart devices.[26]

I'm still trying to work out which side of the fence I sit on. Interestingly, when the American Pew Research Center (a non-partisan organisation which studies issues, attitudes and trends shaping the world) asked some 1150 technology experts, scholars and health specialists the question, 'Over the next decade, how will changes in digital life impact people's overall wellbeing physically and mentally?' here's what they found:

- 47 per cent predicted that individuals' wellbeing will be more helped than harmed by digital life in the next decade.
- 32 per cent said that people's wellbeing will be more harmed than helped.
- 21 per cent predicted there will not be much change in our wellbeing from the way it is now.[27]

I can't predict the future, but one thing I do know is that unless I take charge of my smartphone, the programmers in Silicon Valley – who are being paid to find new and innovative ways to hijack my attention so they can sell it to advertisers – are going to take charge for me.[28]

I've taken a tech-addiction questionnaire that was developed by Professor Mark Griffiths, a behavioural addictions specialist at Nottingham Trent University, who coined the term 'technological addiction' back in the mid-1990s.[29] My score? Six out of 10. By this measure, I *do* have a problem.

PHONE ADDICTION QUESTIONNAIRE

According to Professor Mark Griffiths, answering 'yes' to six or more of the statements below may be indicative of a problematic or addictive smartphone use.

- 'My mobile phone is the most important thing in my life'
- 'Conflicts have arisen between me and my family and/or my partner about the amount of time I spend on my mobile phone'
- 'My mobile phone use often gets in the way of other important things I should be doing (working, education, etc.)'
- 'I spend more time on my mobile phone than almost any other activity'
- 'I use my mobile phone as a way of changing my mood'
- 'Over time I have increased the amount of time I spend on my mobile phone during the day'
- 'If I am unable to use my mobile phone I feel moody and irritable'
- 'I often have strong urges to use my mobile phone'
- 'If I cut down the amount of time I spend on my mobile phone, and then start using it again, I always end up spending as much time on my mobile phone as I did before'
- 'I have lied to other people about how much I use my mobile phone'

Unlike younger millennials (who are regularly slammed in the media for being enslaved to their social feeds and instant notifications), I've always thought that *my* smartphone was used in the name of efficiency, productivity and practical connectivity. This is a wake-up call.

But what to do? As a journalist midway through a documentary self-experiment involving many moving parts, it's not like I can throw my smartphone into Sydney Harbour and saunter off to join the neo-Luddites. The tiny super-computer in the palm of my hand allows me to navigate stress-free to any location, to send a quick message when I'm running late, or have a long video conversation with loved ones overseas. I save hours by doing my online banking, ordering my groceries, or finding spare parts that would once have taken a full day to track down.

One thing that is crystal clear, though, is that if I want to reclaim my attention and set an example for my kids, this is going to take more than willpower alone.

It's Not You, It's Me

Tell me, what is it you plan to do with your one wild and precious life?
— 'The Summer Day', Mary Oliver, 1992[30]

In my work as a health journalist, I estimate that I've read at least 2500 scientific studies top to toe. In all that time, with all that reading, I've never read a study that has truly left me completely, utterly gobsmacked. Until now.

The study was done by a team of researchers at the University of Ulm in Germany and involved looking at how 3000 people used their smartphones. The researchers found that if people didn't have *zeitgebers* (a most magnificent word describing 'time-givers' such as wristwatches and alarm clocks) they had *significantly* less time in their lives for other things.[31] People who reported using both a wristwatch and an alarm clock had an average of 4.71 extra hours in their week. When I did my back-of-the-envelope maths, that amounts to 245 hours, or about 15 (yes, 15!) extra waking days each year.

In the age of overwhelm and overwork, where everyone keeps telling me how they feel more time poor and stressed out than ever before, it's no small thing to be donating 15 days each year to a bottomless feed of clickbait, groundbreaking selfies taken by our work colleagues, and the developmental milestones of other people's children.[32] Just imagine what delights would be possible with a bonus *15 days* each year.

More extraordinarily, the *zeitgebers* study found that people who said that they never used their phone to 'just check' the time had an extra 23.64 hours of leisure in their week compared to people who said they did so very often. That's an extra 23.64 hours each week that they spend playing with their kids, going for walks, being artistic, being scholarly, learning something, nurturing a garden, reading a good book, volunteering their time, or connecting meaningfully with friends.

This is a good news study because it tells me the solution to taking back ownership of my attention may not require having to brick my phone. I may be able to adopt my 'Be Like Batman' strategy, which came to me a few years ago when I was researching a book chapter on diet. Back then it became obvious that the ubiquity, convenience, normalisation and downright deliciousness of junk food makes it impossible to avoid and resist, despite my best intentions to only eat healthy food.

My 'Be Like Batman' strategy is underpinned by the idea that unlike all the other superheroes, Batman has no special powers. He's just a guy who, with the help of his scientifically minded butler Alfred, developed a lot of tools, tricks and techniques that make him *seem* supernatural.

In a similar way, I've developed a tonne of life hacks to fight the evil forces of junk food, including ensuring that healthy food options are easily accessible and appetising, hiding junk food in my laundry and never walking down the confectionery aisle of my supermarket to just 'take a look'.

I can see similarities between my current food diet and my intended technological diet and wonder, could 'Be Like Batman' help me overcome the WMD (Weapon of Mass Distraction) that is my smartphone?

HOW TO BREAK UP WITH MY
JUST-A-BIT-TOO-SMARTPHONE

1. Use a 'dumb' device
I have installed my favourite meditation, audiobook and podcast apps on an old phone, with no email, social media apps, or web browsing enabled. This allows me to indulge in pleasant listening when I'm doing the house cleaning, clothes folding and dishwashing, without using my phone and all its tempting distractions.

---

2. Bring back *zeitgebers* (aka get a wristwatch and an alarm clock)

- An old-school wristwatch will stop me using my smartphone to 'just check' the time, which is often the gateway for getting entrapped in an untended time-wasting vortex.
- I'm using my dumb phone for an alarm clock, which keeps my smartphone out of my bedroom.

3. Make environmental changes

- I've installed a landline (having not had one for years) so that family members will be able to contact me at night in an emergency.
- I've installed smartphone 'beds' in my kitchen at home and on my desk at work where my smartphone will live unseen, unless it is required.

4. Smartphone hacks

- I've restyled my home screen so that it now only has apps that have practical single-use functions such as Maps, Weather, Contacts and ride-hailing apps.
- I have deleted most of my social media apps.
- My email is now buried in a folder on screen three.
- I have set the phone's screen colour profile to greyscale. The apps look far less appealing in shades of grey. Three fast clicks of the home button turns it back to colour if I need it.
- All notifications are disabled without exception, including text message dings and pings.
- I have deleted all games.

5. Getting socially savvy

Until the social media behemoths make a serious commitment to developing useful, ethical products which are not using the 'hook model' to unconsciously manipulate my behaviour and steal my attention, I'm opting out – personally and professionally.

My intention is to only use social media platforms for essential communications with my mother's group, interstate and overseas friends, and my son's preschool class group. Professionally, I'll use social media platforms only as a notice board to alert followers to my new blogs, podcasts and films. I'm taking a leap of faith that people who are interested in my kind of in-depth health journalism will subscribe to my email newsletter, but as marketing guru Seth Godin points out, 'The Mona Lisa has a huge social media presence. Her picture is everywhere. But she doesn't need to tweet.'

Time Well Spent

Before this experiment began, after reading a number of profile pieces of high-achieving executives and elite athletes who swore that mindfulness training boosted their focus and productivity, at the very least I expected this project would put me on that same path. It's now day 182 and the halfway mark of my year of living mindfully experiment and I don't think I'm any better at focusing. I'll have to wait for the results of Neil Bailey's EEG scans for objective data on this, but what I'm learning is just how easily my attention can be stolen.

It's too early to tell if I've managed to kick my tech addiction. As a news junkie I've installed an app called Freedom on my work computer in order to stop myself from accessing distracting websites throughout the workday. So far, I haven't missed anything important and am less frequently tapping my phone screen to check the time, only to emerge several minutes later to the sound of four-year-old Theo repeatedly asking me to join him in his maze drawing game.

By implementing simple technological hacks I estimate that I have quartered the amount of junk information I'm putting into my brain. Although I haven't found any magic extra minutes in my day, it does *feel* like I have more time and I think this is what accounts for my general boost in wellbeing.

In this game of me vs the developers of Silicon Valley, so far I'd say the score is Me: 1, Smartphone: 0.

I wonder what would happen if I turned it *all* off?

CHAPTER SEVEN

Not-Self Help

A few months ago, when I was interviewing the cellular geneticist turned Buddhist monk Matthieu Ricard, I remember looking at the old, bald, robed man across from me and thinking, *Whatever he's on, I want some.* Matthieu was in Australia to give a keynote address on altruism at the world's largest conference on happiness and wellbeing. It was eight in the evening and he was on his fourth and final day of a whirlwind tour, but despite his jet lag, 16-hour workday, and imminent 6.00 a.m. international flight, the 71-year-old's clear blue eyes twinkled with alertness and interest. Far from keeping one eye on the clock, Matthieu brought his undivided attention to our interview as if he had all the time in the world.

Matthieu is famous for being not only the author of a number of bestselling books but also because he earned a place in popular media as the 'happiest man on earth' after neuroscientists published a series of seminal experiments involving his brain.[1] When I met him in person, I didn't need to see the brain scans to know that there was a certain *something* about him. It was as though he radiated a kind of peaceful inner understanding and a readiness for delight, as if he were eternally on the verge of bursting into wise, knowing laughter.

I recently met science journalist Daniel Goleman, who has known Matthieu for years, and he knew exactly what I meant. 'There's a saying in the Tibetan lore, and Matthieu has been in that tradition, they call it "being happy for no reason". That is to say your set point is joyous. It doesn't matter what's happening around you, it just stays like that. So, when you see Matthieu, it's nice just being around him because there's a little contact high from that joy.'

Dan was there in 2004 when neuroscientist Richie Davidson and his team at the Center for Healthy Minds at the University of Wisconsin-Madison first began studying long-term (or 'Olympic level') meditators.[1] Dan recalled watching as Matthieu became the first volunteer to go into the Magnetic Imaging Resonance machine (MRI) when they were developing the protocol. 'Because of some glitches he had to stay in the MRI for about three hours. The MRI is a human cigar box. It's very uncomfortable, clanky and noisy. Some people can't bear it. Matthieu came out after three hours, sat up very cheery, and said, "Oh, that was like a little mini-retreat." In other words, it didn't affect him in the least.'

I interviewed Matthieu at the start of my experiment and confess that I thought it all very well for him to have the happiest brain on the planet; after all, he spends three months every year in a hermitage in the Himalayas, meditating on nothing but kindness and compassion. He doesn't have to deal with the pressure of a mortgage, or deadlines, or production budgets, or traffic, or rude colleagues, or involuntary sleep deprivation caused by young children. As a person living in the *real* world, the chances of me being able to experience anything like Matthieu's level of inner peace were slim to none. But now that I'm past the halfway point of this mindful experiment, I'm starting to reconsider. I wonder if the shift in my internal experience toward more calmness and clarity is a glimpse of what it's like to be inside the mind of the most contented man on earth.

I asked Richie Davidson about this. If I wanted to obtain anything like Matthieu's state of mind, did I need to give up all my worldly possessions and saunter off to meditate in the clear mountain air of Nepal?

'No, I don't think you need to meditate in any specific place,' Richie said. 'What I do believe, based on my own experience as a practitioner, as well as a scientist, is that, that kind of ever-present joy and lightness and spontaneity really comes from long-term practice. I don't think it matters where you practise, but *practice* matters, and our research and other scientists' research is showing that. Moreover, we have new data that's been published that shows that retreat practice makes a different kind of difference compared to daily practice. And retreat practice is really important. Certain kinds of biological changes we see are much more strongly associated with retreat practice than they are with daily practice. Even with two individuals who have identical amounts of overall lifetime practice, the one who had more retreat practice actually shows bigger change.'

Richie was the neuroscientist who first put meditation on the wellbeing science map and his views on the importance of meditation retreat time are echoed by almost every other scientist, every meditation teacher, and every long-term mindfulness practitioner that I've spoken to in the last seven months.

My year of living mindfully is like walking on an unknown forest path. Just as I traipse along to the location I see ahead, a new destination opens up before me and I'm intrigued about what might be around the corner. Curiosity compels me to keep going. Apparently there's something uniquely special about meditating on retreat. I want to know what it is.

It's All Fun and Games Until Someone Loses an 'I'

All is strange to me; I am, as it were, outside my own body and individuality; I am depersonalised, detached, cut adrift. Is this madness?

– Journal of Henri Frédéric Amiel,
19th century Swiss philosopher[2]

My Mindfulness Based Stress Reduction (MBSR) teacher, Tim Goddard, has recommended that I get in touch with a not-for-profit community of meditators known as Melbourne Insight Meditation Group (MIM), who organise weekly meditation groups and 10-day silent retreats to facilitate practising something called vipassanā or insight meditation.

Their website tells me 'a common thread is the focus on settling the mind, developing a level of clarity, and looking carefully at one's experience.' Not to be confused with another kind of popular vipassanā retreat founded by S.N. Goenka, which involves listening to recordings of the long-dead Burmese-Indian businessman, the retreat I've signed up for is being led by Patrick Kearney, a veteran teacher who trained in Asia, the US and Australia and has been leading silent retreats for decades.

I've been told that the retreat might be one of the hardest things I'll ever do, so I'm going into this with my customary level of preparedness. I've read three books offering different retreat perspectives, kept up my daily practice of 45 minutes and done additional homework assigned by Patrick, including switching off the radio when I'm driving and practising silent 'mindful housework' once the kids are in bed each night. But now that my out-of-office email responder is set, my smartphone is off and my kids are on a camping adventure with Jules, despite my readiness and willingness, I can't help but feel some trepidation. I know retreats are not entirely without risk.

I've reread my notes from my conversation a few months ago with Willoughby Britton from Brown University, and was reminded that she founded her non-profit organisation, Cheetah House, in order to support meditators in distress, some of whom experience feelings of 'unreality' and detachment from themselves or the world. This is known as *depersonalisation* or *derealisation*. According to the *British Medical Journal*, this altered state of consciousness is often brought on by adverse life events or severe anxiety. It's thought to act as a kind of natural circuit breaker when life becomes overwhelming.[3] Transient experiences of detachment are surprisingly common, but what often starts as an adaptive, temporary coping mechanism can lead to a chronic disorder. Chronic detachment has also been linked to meditation and stories of the dark side of meditation have dubbed depersonalisation 'enlightenment's evil twin'.[4]

This gives me pause for thought. The goal of my year of living mindfully was not to annihilate my sense of self or detach from those I care about. I'm just looking for ways to suffer a little less and hopefully be a little more present as a mother, sister, wife, daughter, friend and colleague.

As well as Willoughby, I've been assured by two other clinical psychologists who treat meditation-related depersonalisation that I'm not showing any troubling early warning signs and that my retreat experience will likely be safe. 'I think a lot of the quote-unquote "adverse" effects are really about mismatches between the practices and the teachers and the programs, and people's goals,' Willoughby told me. 'People might not want to lose their sense of self, but that's what certain practices are designed to do. So don't do those practices. Do ones that cultivate positive emotions. Those are some of my favourites.'

Despite these reassurances and despite all the planning and preparation, this crazy idea is only starting to hit me now. Why am I doing this? I've never been in a situation where I don't have a book to read, a film to watch, music to listen to, or people to talk to for long periods of time. There's a reason I'm a journalist: I *love* talking to people. Meaningful conversations are as nourishing to me as eating fresh fruit and vegetables. But once we go into what is called 'noble silence', aside from short conversations with Patrick, it will basically be just me and my mind. Why haven't I instead booked a family holiday on the beach in Bali? Or a farm stay with the kids? Or a visit to a health resort where I can indulge in facials and massages?

When time is so precious, why would I *agree* to 10 days in silence with nothing but my unpleasant thoughts and feelings for company?

I put this question to Patrick. 'Have you ever come back from a holiday thinking, *I need a holiday to recover?* The simple answer is that at the end of your retreat, you will feel much better than you would have felt after 10 days on the beach in Bali,' he said reassuringly over Skype.

HOW TO FIND A MINDFULNESS TEACHER

Five questions to ask

1. Where did you learn meditation?
The expert teachers I've met have usually been trained by someone, who trained with someone, who trained with someone else, going back hundreds if not thousands of years. This is sometimes called a meditation 'lineage'. Although some teachers might have their own unique style, there's a great deal to be gained by being grounded in time-tested techniques. I look for teachers who have clearly done their own hard yards; those who have been meditating for decades – not weeks or months – and who still study, train and attend long retreats to further their own practice.

2. Where did you receive your teacher training?
Although there's not a universal mindfulness teacher 'qualification', this is a helpful question. In the same way that I wouldn't want to learn yoga from someone who attended a few

yoga classes, or to receive psychotherapy from someone who went to see a psychologist a few times for their own problems, I look for teachers who are trained or certified by a well-regarded institution. A good follow-up question is, 'Who encouraged you to become a mindfulness teacher?' It might be a red flag if they can't articulate a person or an institution with a good reputation.

3. Is your style about relaxation or acceptance?

This simple question tells me if they're teaching *mindfulness* meditation. I now know that even though mindfulness meditation can be relaxing, that is not the main game. One of the actual aims is to change the way I relate to my thoughts, feelings and experiences by cultivating non-judgemental awareness. If the teacher is not making that clear then they may not understand mindfulness themselves.

4. Do you think everyone should meditate?

Although a good mindfulness teacher might say they *wish* everyone practised, they will also be able to give a nuanced, thoughtful response which touches on the fact that although mindfulness meditation *can* help many people in varying circumstances, it is certainly not for everyone. In fact, they may also say that there are some people who *shouldn't* try mindfulness.

5. What is your motivation to teach?

Mindfulness teachers who are the real deal are likely to say they want to help people to understand the nature of their own minds better. They will want to hold the space and offer guidance to help others navigate the tricky waters of their own minds. They will encourage independent thinking and open inquiry in their students. Red flags would be signs of pushiness, the requirement of blind obedience, or the expectation of adulation.

Into The Void

I came to this experiment through the lens of science-based health journalism. In the absence of any other solutions, I was interested in gaining proficiency in mindfulness meditation for its possible mental and physical health benefits rather than wanting to acquire spiritual insight or attainment. I guess it was more of an existential quest rather than a spiritual one. As such, until now I've been more concerned with what contemporary scientists think mindfulness is and does, and how it works, rather than its ancient historical roots. But in the interest of rigorous enquiry (personal curiosity) it's necessary to examine the historical foundations for my retreat curriculum.

According to *Mindfulness in Plain English* by Buddhist monk Henepola Gunaratana (or 'Bhante G' to Westerners like me who struggle with foreign names), the ancient Pāli term for insight meditation is *vipassanā bhavana*. Vipassanā is derived from two root words: *vi*, which means either 'special' or 'clear', and *passanā*, which means 'seeing' or 'perceiving'. The word *bhavana* comes from the root word *bhu*, which means 'to grow' or 'to become' and implies mental cultivation, or meditation. So, in Bhante G's plain English, apparently I've signed up to a retreat which teaches 'looking into something with clarity and precision, seeing each component as distinct and separate, and piercing all the way through so as to perceive the most fundamental reality of that thing.'[5] (Is it just me or does this sound like both science *and* journalism? Something tells me that this vipassanā path I'm on is the right one for me.)

Although I'm not naturally inclined towards religion, the research brief on my retreat would be incomplete without looking a little deeper into its Buddhist origins.

As the story goes, Siddhārtha Gautama was an ancient Indian prince, with access to no less than three palaces (spring, winter *and* summer), when he abandoned his privileged position in order to find a balm for what he called his *suffering*. Nowadays we might diagnose Siddhārtha's #firstworldproblems as a midlife crisis or clinical depression (Patrick thinks his 'issues' were more akin to being an angst-ridden adolescent) but, in any case, the miserable prince gave it all up in order to study how his mind worked, transcend his dissatisfaction, then share what he learned with others.[6]

From a secular point of view, Siddhārtha grew up to be a very knowledgeable guy who taught others how to suffer less by understanding the nature of their mind. And it turned out, what he taught *really* took off. You could say he was kind-of the world's first, bestselling psychologist.

Centuries later there was a religion called Buddhism, but it was mostly about trying to live a wholesome life, and the idea of practising meditation in order to obtain enlightenment like Siddhārtha was something left to celibate monks who were willing to abandon all their worldly possessions.

That all started to change in Burma in the late 19th century, when everyone was worried that Buddhism would be lost because the Burmese King (who was the chief philanthropic sponsor of monasteries and monks) was exiled by the British Empire. For the first time, the laity mobilised to start Buddhism clubs and associations. Some of the really articulate monks became similar to rock star motivational speakers and, like olden-day incarnations of Tony Robbins, could attract tens of thousands of people to public events. As 'Buddhism-Made-Simple' pamphlets started spreading like TED talks on Facebook, mindfulness meditation became something for everyone to try.

One of Patrick's principal teachers was a popular monk named Mahāsī Sayādaw who, in the mid-1950s (during Burma's next political upheaval, when the newly independent government wanted to unite the country by turbo-charging widespread cultural Buddhism), got sponsored by the Burmese prime minister.[7,8] Although his name sounds exotic, *mahāsī* actually translates to 'big drum' in English and *sayādaw* is the Burmese honorific for teaching monks. So, basically, Mahāsī Sayādaw was a monk who first started teaching at a monastery that had a big drum.

Anyhow, the English-speaking Mahāsī travelled extensively abroad, including through the US, UK and Europe, and his 'Mahāsī method' became one of the foremost influences on many teachers popularising mindfulness in the West today. The appeal to secular-minded Westerners like me is that the method is largely drawn from an ancient text called the *Satipatthana Sutta*, or the *Foundations of Mindfulness* – one of, if not the earliest records of the Buddha's lessons, which outlines exactly *how* to meditate and doesn't depict Siddhārtha as possessing any special omniscient or spiritual powers.[9]

So, Mahāsī taught his method to a pool of trained teachers, one of whom was another monk named U Pandita. U Pandita trained Patrick. And Patrick is now about to train me ...

Just A Thought

The retreat was held in Kallara, nestled in the foothills of the Strathbogie Ranges in Victoria; a bushland wonderland in mid-winter, with winding forest paths shrouded in mist, and home to kangaroos, koalas and soaring wedge-tailed eagles.

Most days started at 5.30 a.m. and ended at 9.00 p.m. By day three I was in a self-managed rhythm of sitting in meditation for 45 minutes and then moving in meditation for 45 minutes, interrupted only by twice daily lectures from Patrick, meal times, and my assigned daily mindful work task of cleaning the communal toilets and showers. (I'm told other styles of vipassanā retreat can be much more strict.)

Although I'm still a beginner in comparison to the more seasoned meditators (in all their splendid diversity, from their beehive hairdos to their bald heads, their hiking boots and high heels, their cashmere sweaters, Nepalese knits and holey sweatpants), it is perhaps because I'd been training for this solitary marathon for 219 days that I seemed to fare better in the silence than others.

On the eighth afternoon one singularly agitated woman, who had become increasingly troubled as the days went by, paced our

communal lounge room in search of anything, *anything* other than being in the company of her own mind. Eventually, she took to reading the torn-out classified section of a six-month-old newspaper waiting by the fireside for use as kindling. I watched as her palpable mental torment sent ripples through the still room. Although I knew she was in good hands with Patrick, I felt my own heart sending a compassionate reply to her suffering.

DAILY RETREAT NOTES

DAY 1

Wait, why am I doing this again?

DAY 2

The voice in my head is REALLY loud. It's like blah blah blah blah blah *constantly.*

DAY 3

Argh. I'm not getting any better at focusing my distracted mind.

DAY 4

All this sitting = pain. And yet, it isn't bothering me. I can even sometimes turn it up and down by using my attention. Meditation = a form of *miiind control.*

DAY 5

Pain is just weakness leaving the body. LOL. Just kidding. Dinner bell. Got to go.

DAY 6

My mind is settling. Actually the silence is quite nice.

DAY 7

In deep absorption, I see there is only a continual remembering of what just happened.

DAY 8

For increasingly longer periods I can witness the unfolding of my experience moment, by moment, by moment. OMG, I'm starting to sound like Jon Kabat-Zinn!

DAY 9

I finally get it. Mindfulness is not the same as the noun *awareness*. It is the practice of 'aware-ing'. Paying attention to unfolding experience. And when I'm able to sustain it, all the blah blah blah ceases. It's like a holiday from myself. I've been searching for this my whole life.

DAY 10

I'm starting to get a glimpse of what inner peace feels like.

Noticings Per Minute

Over the 10 days of my retreat, Patrick methodically guided me through a series of mental exercises designed to increasingly focus my concentration and reveal how my mind works in forensic detail. He first instructed me how to choose an appropriate 'object' of my awareness (such as my breath, a bodily sensation, or a sense such as taste or touch) then gave me detailed instructions on how to anchor my attention there.

As the days went by and my distractible mind began to settle, he showed me how to overcome my mental obstacles and tweak my practice in order to pay *even* closer attention to these objects of awareness; to experience the taste of food in minute detail, to track the sensations of the forest under my feet; to *hear* myself thinking from moment to moment to moment, without being caught up in the thoughts themselves.

This is something that one of Patrick's contemporaries, an American mindfulness teacher named Joseph Goldstein (who also trained in the Mahāsi method), calls NPMs or 'Noticings Per Minute'. 'In the beginning, our NPMs are pretty low, maybe 10 or 20. But as we cultivate awareness and mindfulness, the NPMs go way up and we see within a breath, or within a step, so many different, changing sensations happening. And we also see the changing nature in our minds, the rapidity of thoughts arising and passing,' Joseph told the author of *Why Buddhism is True*, Robert Wright.[10,11]

So, having been given expert instruction by Patrick and being freed from the normal mental complexities of my life's usual social interactions, practicalities and distractions, I was eventually able to track my awareness with greater precision for extended periods of time. And then, like peering closely at a rainbow only to find that it's actually a beautiful illusion of light dispersed in water droplets, my mind's constructed reality was revealed. This revelation is, I'm pretty sure, what Siddhārtha was getting at 2500 years ago.

MEDITATION JOURNAL, DAY 225

Vipassanā Meditation Retreat, Day 6
5.30 a.m.–9.00 p.m. x 10 days

Time: *12.30 p.m.*
Method: *Mindful eating*
Technique: *Concentration. Paying attention to the moment 'I choose'.*

Experiment notes:
Viewed with a wide-angle lens, I am sitting in silence, eating a
garden salad. Viewed in more close-up detail, I am experiencing
eating a leaf. The crispness. Crunchiness. Sliminess. In extreme
close-up, the next forkful of salad is poised to enter my mouth. I
witness the feeling of intention arise. The intention to eat. I follow
the subsequent sensations in my chest, arm and wrist as I move
to bring the fork to my mouth. I note how the mental intention
to eat gave rise to the physical movement towards my mouth. But
my observation of the process disrupts the continuity and the
food remains poised to be eaten. I am waiting for the moment
my intention to eat will change to actually eating. When will the
decision arise? I'm waiting … waiting … waiting. While ever I
watch for the choice to arise, nothing happens. It's as if I'm frozen
in time. A thought occurs. How long has it been? I notice the
arising of the thought. Then, I am eating the lettuce. There was no
decision. Or if there was, I didn't know about it. It just happened
on its own. It was as though the thought about time passing gave
rise to the action to eat. There was no choice. There was no me.
It happened on its own. How many decisions do I 'think' I make
every day that actually happen on their own like this?

By day 10, the revelations or *insights* about the nature of my mind that arose from this kind of micro-examination of my moment-to-moment experience were revelatory, and uniquely peaceful. During periods of experiential absorption, a particular kind of self-referential thinking – a habitual *me, myself* and *mine* narrative – fell away. All the wonderings about what things mean for *me*, all the planning for *my* future and ruminating on *my* past; all the protecting of *myself* and the telling of stories to *myself* a hundred thousand million times a day – all that made way for windows of equanimity, abiding inner peace and a sense of connectedness, of oneness, with all things.

Aside from saying 'yes' to Jules when he proposed marriage and becoming a mother to our two adventurous boys, the retreat was the best thing I've ever done.

What are my chances of making it to day 365 of this experiment now? 99 per cent.

CHAPTER EIGHT

From Me to We

The human brain has 100 billion neurons, each neuron connected to ten thousand other neurons. So, believe it or not, sitting on your shoulders is the most complex object in the known universe.

– American theoretical physicist Michio Kaku talking to
WNYC radio host Leonard Lopate[1]

A scientist wanting to study the effects of the retreat on my physical and mental health would have difficulty extracting its active ingredients. Was it the healthy vegetarian meals, mindful forest walks, or early morning yoga that caused my deep sense of inner wellbeing? Perhaps it was the good nights of sleep or the absence of stress and parenting pressures? Or was it the 126 hours of meditation?

I've been home for a month and am wondering what neuroscientists have to say about the feeling of wellbeing that's come over me. Surprisingly little, it turns out. Despite tens of thousands of researchers dedicating time and energy to figuring out what brains do and how they work; despite the impressive technology that enables neuroscientists to peer inside our skulls; and despite having discovered more about our grey matter in the last 20 years than in all prior human history, the notion of 'conscious awareness' is still only theoretical.[2–5]

It also turns out that the old 'triune brain' model, which pits a primitive 'lizard brain' against more recently evolved 'mammal' and 'executive' human parts, was debunked more than 20 years ago.[6] And while it was once thought that brain functions could be attributed to the isolated operations in single brain areas, despite what I was told by my high school maths teacher – that I should stick to English because I'm a 'right-brained' creative thinker rather than a logic-driven 'left-brained' type – activity is similar on both sides, regardless of personality.

It is true that some brain functions have been found to reside more on one side than the other, but the left and right hemispheres are deeply interconnected.[7] In fact, evidence suggests that mental activity results from complicated, dynamic *interactions* of brain areas that operate in large-scale networks.[8] Basically, my brain's 100 billion neurons work together to form a matrix of globalised, Internet-like complexity.

With the lens of someone who's now been meditating daily for 275 days, I went back to my notes from my interview with Associate Professor Amishi Jah from the University of Miami. I interviewed Amishi when I was still setting up my mindful experiment and in the throes of enlisting the support of every scientist I could think of. I thought that it would just be a matter of hopping into an MRI and putting on an EEG cap and the neuroscientists would be able to tell me if mindfulness 'worked' for me. As a result, I didn't fully take in the significance of what

Amishi meant when she tried to explain that we're nowhere near having what the scientists call a 'brain signature' for mindfulness.

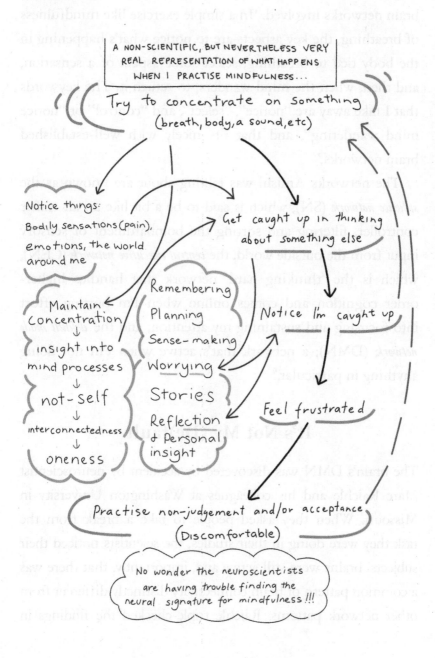

A NON-SCIENTIFIC, BUT NEVERTHELESS VERY REAL REPRESENTATION OF WHAT HAPPENS WHEN I PRACTISE MINDFULNESS...

Try to concentrate on something
(breath, body, a sound, etc)

Notice things:
Bodily sensations (pain), emotions, the world around me

Get caught up in thinking about something else

Remembering
Planning
Sense-making
Worrying
Stories
Reflection & Personal insight

Maintain Concentration
↓
insight into mind processes
↓
not-self
↓
interconnectedness
↓
oneness

Notice I'm caught up

Feel frustrated

Practise non-judgement and/or acceptance
(Discomfortable)

No wonder the neuroscientists are having trouble finding the neural signature for mindfulness !!!

We are only just beginning to understand what happens in our head when we meditate and when, where and for whom it might be beneficial. Amishi thinks there are *at least* three major brain networks involved. 'In a simple exercise like mindfulness of breathing, the key aspects are to notice what's happening in the body tied to breathing, select some aspect of a sensation, and then, when the mind wanders, to return it. The keywords that I take away are "notice", "select", and "control" or "notice mind wandering", and that fits nicely with well-established brain networks.'

The networks Amishi was talking about are known as the *salience network* (SN), which is said to be a bit like an air traffic controller, filtering and sorting the bombardment of sensory input from the outside world; the *central executive network* (CEN), which is the 'thinking hard' network that handles higher-order cognition and comes online when I'm putting effort into focusing and sustaining my attention; and the *default mode network* (DMN), a network that's active when I'm not doing anything in particular.[9]

It's Not My (De)fault

The brain's DMN was discovered by accident by neuroscientist Marc Raichle and his colleagues at Washington University in Missouri. When they asked people to take a break from the task they were doing in their studies, the scientists noticed their subjects' brains were still active and, importantly, that there was a common pattern of brain connectivity distinctly different from other network patterns. Raichle triple-checked the findings in follow-up studies and several years later went public, coining the term 'default mode' in 2001.[10]

Since then, scientists all over the world have been trying to work out what our brain does when it's not supposed to be doing anything. It turns out we automatically default to thinking about ourselves and our place within the world.[11] The DMN's job is to contemplate, understand, imagine, and make sense of all things related to 'me', 'myself' and 'I'.

Researchers think that subsystems within the DMN are crucial for creating everything from a static 'narrative self' (*I am Shannon*), to episodic memories (*I remember the day I lost my first tooth* ...), to enabling me to embark on a journey of mental time travel (*I wish I didn't say that*, or *this is how I'll say it next time*), to enabling me to 'mentalise' (develop complex understandings of myself and others), and have a 'theory of mind', which is an ability to imagine someone else's inner world (*I imagine that she's feeling really disappointed right now*).[12,13]

This all sounds rather complicated, but social cognitive scientist Matthew Lieberman from the University of California, Los Angeles thinks that the DMN makes perfect sense from an evolutionary point of view. In his book *Social: Why Our Brains Are Wired to Connect*, Lieberman explains that being pre-programmed to spend our 'downtime' processing and reprocessing social information and making sense of our interactions is Mother Nature's way of ensuring that we'll spend our lives motivated by strong social connection, which is good for our survival as a species.

In fact, the DMN has been shown to be active in babies as young as two weeks old, who can't even smile or intentionally move their own hands yet. By the time they're two years old, their DMNs are similar to an adult's.[14] Lieberman's conclusion is that in the same way we have basic needs for food, water and shelter, we also have a basic need for connectedness.[15]

Although good for humankind, there's a huge downside to having an inner social network. Just like Mark Zuckerberg's social *media* network, it's notorious for hijacking my inner thoughts and taking me off task. Whenever I replay conversations in my head or rewrite my verbal faux pas, whenever I sink into scenes from childhood or catapult myself into horrible hypothetical futures, whenever I obsess over which of two new rugs to buy for my living room or if the red blouse will work for my upcoming presentation, whenever I craft imaginary dialogues or subject myself to an inner moral performance review and analyse what I could be doing better, that's all my DMN switching on.[16]

One famous study called 'A Wandering Mind is an Unhappy Mind' asked thousands of people to report their mental focus and mood at random times throughout the day. It concluded that people are thinking about what is *not* happening almost as often as they are thinking about what *is* happening. The researchers also concluded that doing so generally makes people unhappy.[17]

Mother Nature didn't intend for my default self-system to make me happy all the time; she designed it to automatically force me to mull over my life. No wonder I found the simple mindful dishwashing homework assignment set by Patrick in preparation for the retreat an absolute chore. By foregoing my usual audiobook entertainment while scraping congealed dinosaur pasta off the bottom of a saucepan, my brain wanted to default to thinking about all the problems in my life: my difficult relationships, my worries for the future and anxieties about the past.

It's also little wonder that when I experienced a state of deep absorption in moment-to-moment awareness while I was on the retreat – a place that was free of all this me me *me* thinking – it felt as though I'd found inner rest and relaxation. It was like I'd taken a holiday ... from myself.

I have a whole new appreciation for why people like Jules enjoy sports such as mountaineering. When he's on those huge mountains, being able to concentrate on where he places each hand and foot is a matter of life or death. There's not much use for incessant self-focused chatter in that situation.

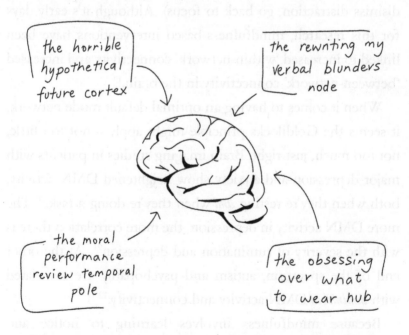

the horrible hypothetical future cortex

the rewriting my verbal blunders node

the moral performance review temporal pole

the obsessing over what to wear hub

THE NETWORKS OF MY MEDITATING BRAIN

M ndfulness

Although there are currently no precise 'neural signatures' for mental illnesses, characteristics such as intense emotionality, excessive worry, rumination, self-criticism and loneliness are hallmarks of the default network. Neuroscientists have linked abnormal default activity to a range of distress disorders from depression, anxiety and post-traumatic stress to attention deficit disorder and autism.[18] So it's here that, yet again, mindfulness training enters the picture.

Mindfulness is kind of like a cognitive-yoga or an inner mental workout, which trains us to constantly toggle between brain networks (focus, get distracted, observe distraction, dismiss distraction, go back to focus). Although it's early days for this research, mindfulness-based interventions have been linked to increased 'within-network' connectivity and increased 'between-network' connectivity in the brain.[19]

When it comes to having an optimal default mode network, it seems the Goldilocks principle might apply – not too little, not too much, just right. Brain imaging studies in patients with major depression and anxiety show heightened DMN activity, both when they're resting *and* when they're doing a task.[20] The more DMN activity in depression, the more correlation there is with the severity of rumination and depression[21]. At the other end of the spectrum, autism and psychopathy are associated with *diminished* DMN activity and connectivity.[22]

Because mindfulness involves learning to notice and differentiate from self-related thoughts (*I am angry* vs *huh, there is anger*), in 2011 Judson Brewer, who was then at Yale University, wondered if it's possible that mindfulness training could nudge our default mode activity towards being more present-centred, and possibly happier.

Jud used functional MRI to assess the brains of 12 experienced meditators, with an average of 10 565 hours of practice under their belts, and compared them to 13 novices. It transpired that the default networks of long-term meditators were very different to novices. During three types of meditation practice – focused awareness (focusing on a meditation 'object' such as breath coming in and out), open awareness (a more advanced technique of tracking whatever happens in awareness moment to moment) and loving kindness (intentionally thinking kind and loving thoughts about oneself, others and the world) – Jud found that the DMN in the expert meditators was significantly less activated than beginners. This was particularly true when they practised loving-kindness meditation.[23]

Remarkable DMN connectivity has also been recorded in mindfulness meditators with an average of 9040 hours of practice under their belts, in Zen meditators with an average of 1709 hours of practice, and even in groups of elderly people who took part in an eight-week mindfulness course.[24–27]

Perhaps an even more interesting finding from Jud's research is that meditators with the training equivalent of Olympic athletes also show less activated default networks when they were *not* doing a task like meditating, particularly in a DMN 'hub' called the posterior cingulate cortex (PCC), which is kind of like the Central Station of the default network.[28,29]

Jud has since demonstrated that when highly experienced meditators report being in states of absorption, which they described as 'undistracted awareness', 'observing sensory experience', and 'effortless doing', their PCCs get *really* quiet.[30]

'I feel like we're just scratching the surface here, but the PCC seems to be a marker of the experiential self. At least, that's our hypothesis,' Jud told me after a lot of careful preamble in order to not oversell this remarkable finding. 'When somebody's been meditating for a long time, those boundaries between the self and the rest of the world can start to dissolve. And on an experiential level, we feel this often as an expanding quality of our experience. And if that expansion goes all the way to infinity, we start to lose that boundary between ourselves and others.'

Richie Davidson and Dan Goleman both told me that they think Jud's study is indicative of their pet theory that, over time, with regular practice, mindfulness has long-lasting trait effects rather than transient state effects. 'It's a good sign, after all these meditators intentionally train in order to be as mindful in their daily lives as during meditation sessions,' Dan said.

In the same way that strength exercises don't only make my muscles stronger when I'm at the gym (workouts also help when I'm doing things like picking up Izzy and bringing in armfuls of groceries from the car), Jud is on the way towards finding one of the neural fingerprints that show mindfulness training on the meditation stool carries over into my everyday life as well. This will be an area of research to keep a close eye on in the future.

All this is not to say that taking a break and allowing my default mode to wander around is a *bad* thing. Indeed, mental time out has been shown to help brains practise what they've recently learned and to facilitate creative insights.[31,32] When I'm in the thick of researching and writing complex ideas, I regularly need to stop and allow my mind to go on autopilot by going for a walk or taking a shower. In fact, I worked out how to intelligibly explain the DMN to others only after I'd allowed my attention to wander. The evidence shows that's not uncommon.[33]

It's not that my 'self' itself is the problem (it's *really* useful to be able to remember who I am each morning), rather, the problem is the *extent* to which I get caught up in the drama of my life and take it personally when something happens to me, good or bad.

As I discovered in the early weeks of this experiment, mindfulness training strengthens my ability to 'decentre' – to observe things that arise in my mind (such as thoughts, feelings and memories) from a healthy psychological stance, with greater awareness and a new perspective. All these months later, I can now observe – for example, as I wash the dishes night after night – that I'm often thinking the same things over and over again, and then choose what I might or might not do with that observation.

Ron Purser's 'McMindfulness' criticisms raised the possibility that all this non-judging and self-distancing could turn me into a cold and indifferent drone, but what I've found is that by being better able to observe the grasping version of me, the wanting version of me, the needing version of me, I am more open to my own experience and to the experiences of others. In that openness, I'm better able to approach other people's suffering. In fact, my experience seems to be the opposite of what Purser warned could happen. Rather than becoming an automaton, I'm more aware than ever of my thoughts and behaviours – and how they affect others. This reminds me of my conversation with Jon Kabat-Zinn at the start of this project, before I began meditating every day. I wanted to know his response to people who thought that setting time aside each day to meditate was a selfish endeavour.

'The cliché of course is if the oxygen masks in a plane drop down, you first put it on yourself before you even put it on your child because if you [pass] out, you're not going to be of use to anybody else. [The idea is that] if you take care of your own instrument you're not doing it for yourself ... you're doing it for, in some sense, the sake of the world. Now that sounds imbecilic or just sort of pie in the sky, but there's a truth in it because the world is interconnected. When you have one locus of sanity in the world, or more, that's going to affect the entire world,' he responded.

What Would Happen If Everyone Truly Believed Everything Is One?

Say I Am You

I am dust particles in sunlight.
I am the round sun.

To the bits of dust I say, Stay.
To the sun, Keep moving.

I am morning mist,
and the breathing of evening.

I am wind in the top of a grove,
and surf on the cliff.

Mast, rudder, helmsman, and keel,
I am also the coral reef they founder on.

I am a tree with a trained parrot in its branches.
Silence, thought, and voice.

The musical air coming through a flute,
a spark of a stone, a flickering in metal.

Both candle,
and the moth crazy around it.

Rose, and the nightingale
lost in the fragrance.

I am all orders of being, the circling galaxy,
the evolutionary intelligence, the lift,
and the falling away.

What is,
and what isn't.

You who know Jelaluddin,
You the one in all,

Say who I am. Say I am You.

> – Jelaluddin Muhammad Rūmī (aka 'Rumi')
> 13th-century Persian poet[34]

We experience ourselves, our thoughts and feelings as something separate from the rest. A kind of optical delusion of consciousness.

> – Albert Einstein[35]

The Austrian quantum physicist and 1933 winner of the Nobel Prize in Physics, Erwin Schrödinger, is perhaps best known for a thought experiment involving an animal. Schrödinger imagined taking a cat and putting it in a sealed box in which a device had a 50 per cent chance of killing the cat in the next hour. At the end of the hour, he asked, what happened to the cat?

Common sense suggests that the cat is either alive or dead. But Schrödinger pointed out that the instant before the box is open, the cat is actually equal parts alive or dead ... at the *same* time. According to quantum physics, it's only when the box is opened that we see what happened. Until then, the cat's fate is a haze of probability – half one thing, half the other.[36]

This mind-bending thought experiment is difficult to wrap my head around but that was Schrödinger's point. His cat is often used to spark conversations about the ultimate reality of the universe beyond our perception and to highlight that, despite the topic usually being left to the province of religious, spiritual, philosophical or cultural discussions, even quantum physicists think that there is a 'oneness' of the universe beyond what we perceive in time and space.

Since coming home from the retreat, there was one occasion where my mindfulness practice became another form of mind-bending experiment.

MEDITATION JOURNAL, DAY 281

Time: *45 minutes daily*
Method: *Self-guided meditation*
Technique: *Mental noting*

Experiment notes:
Nothing to do, nowhere to be, just here, now. Start with breath. In. Out. Mental activity. Aware. A new quality of mind. Curiosity. Investigating. Body dissolving. No me. No other. No time. No space. Unbounded eternity. Everything and nothing. Awareness itself. Just awake and aware. Peaceful and joyful. Understanding. Compassionate. Knowing.

I describe my experience on day 281 as being a little like my car. Ordinarily, it's clear that there's a car parked in my garage. I can turn on the engine and drive it from A to B and everyone I know recognises my car when it approaches. But if I look closer at my car — at the steering wheel, or tyres, or even the engine under the bonnet – I see that although these individual parts are separately and in their own way necessary, no individual part could be said to *be* my car. The whole is literally greater than the sum of its (car) parts.

In the same way, when I use an extreme close-up lens to objectively examine my inner mental world, witnessing the transient streams of thought, memories, sensations and perceptions, the concept of 'me' disappears, along with time and space, leaving only a sense of expansive oneness. The experience is fleeting but has a great effect on my perception of the true nature of things and my place within it.

There's an interesting paradox at work here. Evolutionary forces designed my brain to default to think about 'me' whenever it could so that I'd get along better with others. However, through meditation training, when this default mode is turned down, I experience a feeling of greater connectedness and wellbeing.

Researchers Kate Diebels and Mark Leary from Duke University in North Carolina were the first to examine the impact of a belief in 'oneness' as a separate belief from things such as sacredness or having a relationship with God. Not surprisingly, they found that people who scored higher on their 'Belief in Oneness Scale' were more likely to have concern for the welfare of other people, animals and nature, and that oneness believers were more likely to feel that people share common problems and shortcomings. They concluded that believing in oneness has broad implications for our personal, social, cultural, political and environmental wellbeing.[37]

This makes sense to me. When I focus on myself, my world contracts as my own problems and preoccupations loom large. Being self-focused mutes my empathy and my compassion. But when I focus on connectedness, my world expands, my own problems drift to the periphery and my capacity for presence and compassionate action increases.

Interestingly, in the 'Psychological Implications of Believing that Everything is One' study, believing in the harmony of all things did not relate to how much people prioritised their own concerns, which tells me that caring deeply for the world outside of my own self-interest is not in opposition to self-care, healthy boundaries and personal life goals. I've since uncovered two other large-scale studies involving around 7000 and 70000 people respectively, which found that regardless of religious stance, a belief in oneness is associated with having greater life satisfaction.[38]

I wonder how long my post-retreat sense of inner wellbeing will last. Despite meditating every day since coming home, the effects are starting to fade. My 'blah-blah-blah-story-of-me' networks are once again starting to dominate my conscious experience. My states of deep connectedness are becoming far less frequent and less enduring.

I recall a conversation I had with Patrick during our final student–teacher session. I asked him how I could possibly keep this feeling going back in the real world. 'You can't,' was his succinct answer. 'You need all the conditions to come together. That's why people do retreats. Now, insight meditation is interesting in that it has a characteristic that once you see something, you've seen it and that never goes away.'

'So I'm not going to forget?' I asked.

'You will forget your insights, but the effect that it has – "Oh, this is what's going on" – that stays. I like to call it the Santa Claus effect. So when we're young and every year this magical figure turns up (we always left out some beer for him and some cake because by the time he gets to Australia he's pretty tired) and then one Christmas Eve, you hear sounds in the living room, so you creep out and have a look and there's your father scoffing the beer and your mother laying out the presents. After that, Christmas can never be the same because you've seen something and the world is different now. Insight works like this. You forget your insight, but there's a sense that your insight never forgets you.'

I'm now 291 days into my mindfulness experiment and quite surprised that this story is no longer moving towards a soaring climax in which I discover my own scientific results and find out if mindfulness is 'worth it'. In the beginning I wanted *proof* – one way or another – if mindfulness training could improve my health and wellbeing. But although I'm still curious to know what will be discovered, the scientific results have become significantly less important. With my mindfulness oxygen mask fitted firmly, my own problems seem less significant and I feel more able to turn my full attention to the suffering of others.

I'm ready to tackle the other big question that inspired this project: could mindfulness be part of the solution for our mental health crisis? Can it really ease the suffering of anyone, anywhere, in any circumstances? My eyes are now open, more so than ever, to the need to offer more concrete recommendations for all people, on the full spectrum of the mental wellbeing continuum. But the truth is, as an educated white woman living in a peaceful country … even at this late stage in the game, I still don't know if mindfulness is a *universal* answer, let alone *the* answer.

I've received a grant that allows me to make one final international trip before the project finishes. While I've come across plenty of new potential case studies to explore – of mindfulness being used to help people in situations very different to my own, such as in prisons, in disadvantaged schools and impoverished communities – my attention has been drawn to the Middle East and to the frontline of the global humanitarian crisis. If there was ever a place to put mindfulness to the test, this would be it …

CHAPTER NINE

Moments of Refuge

MEDITATION JOURNAL, DAY 317

Time: *45 minutes*

Method: *Self-guided meditation*

Technique: *Open Awareness using Insight Timer app*

Experiment notes:

I am on a plane from Sydney, bound for Amman, Jordan. No
emails can be sent. No calls can be made. Just me and my
mind. I've set the timer and am settling in. My attention goes
to the cold air coming from above me. The air conditioner is
my primary object of awareness. Coldness. Unpleasantness.
Disliking. Within moments my thoughts are elsewhere. My
mind is in automatic sense-making mode; taking stock of all
that has happened and all that has been learned in the last
few full-on days. Filming permit difficulties, visa issues, my
last-minute eight-hour drive to reclaim my passport from
the Jordanian embassy, the sewerage pipe under our house
bursting ... When the thoughts that need to be thought

---

have been thought, my attention drifts back to the coolness of the air conditioner above. A young child is crying. It's as if her cries reach inside me and take hold of my heart. I am tender after saying goodbye to my own kids. There is palpable heartache. Her cries become high-pitched squeals. Is she in pain? Energy pulses through me. I want to go to the child. But she is not mine. Her mother is there. She is soothed. She loses momentum and downshifts into a wail. I watch, fascinated by her call and my automatic internal response. Call and response. Call and response. Call and response. She settles. I have no sense of her. Is she asleep? Our connection is broken. I become aware of my noticing. My wondrous ability to notice a microscopic experience like this. Back to my object of awareness. Cold air conditioning above me. Unpleasantness. Disliking. Now I am bored. I want to watch a movie. When was the last time I got to sit and watch a movie? Weeks ago? Months ago? I look at the meditation timer on my app. Am I there yet? How much longer? Ha! Even now, 316 days in, I still have an aversion to having to meditate.

Forcibly Displaced

Having filmed in locations all over the globe, from first-class hotels to developing-world slums, I knew shooting in the Middle East would involve long days, difficult work, cultural obstacles and things not going to plan. I'd done my best to prepare: I'd spoken to aid workers and other journalists who'd been there, done risk assessments and background checks, and tracked down the best local guide in the business. But despite my efforts, nothing could have prepared me for the sprawling Za'atari refugee camp on the border of Jordan and Syria.

Za'atari is a two-hour drive from my hotel base in Jordan's capital, Amman, and quite literally in the middle of nowhere; a dusty, barren and unforgiving desert of rock and gravel. It's one of the most arid places on the planet, with poor quality soil, blistering summer days that reach 45° Celsius and icy winters that include prolonged periods of snow and temperatures below zero. No one would choose to live here, unless they absolutely had to. Those who do have reluctantly come from Syria, mostly the city of Dara'a.

In March 2011, Dara'a became known as the 'Cradle of the Revolution' after community protests started when 15 teenage boys were arrested and tortured for painting anti-government graffiti on their school wall. The Syrian government's brutal response to relatively minor pro-democracy protests fanned the flames of a national uprising, including the emergence of disparate militant opposition groups, armed rebellion and a full-scale civil war. The war is now in its seventh year, with no end in sight, and has claimed the lives of more than 500 000 people and displaced almost 12 million others.[1,2]

As the conflict escalated, Za'atari, which is about 40 kilometres south of the now destroyed city of Dara'a, emerged almost overnight. What began as a pop-up tent camp in 2012 has transformed into one of the largest refugee settlements in the world, a pseudo-city that is home to around 80 000 people. Thanks to the efforts of the United Nations High Commissioner for Refugees (UNHCR) and the Jordanian government, families survive in some 15000 ramshackle caravans made from corrugated iron and fibro. They have access to water wells spread throughout the camp, as well as solar-generated electricity for a few hours a day.

The sheer scale of the camp struck me to my core. The aerial drone that Chris Bland, my cinematographer, put in the air for our documentary couldn't get high enough to capture the full extent of the camp. Tragically, Za'atari represents only a *fraction* of the more than 70 million displaced people around the world, many of whom make do in urban slums without the protection of the UNHCR.[3] Ihab Mustaseb, my English-speaking guide, told me repeatedly that people in Za'atari 'have it good' compared to the hundreds of thousands living in Amman.

With our location shots complete, Ihab took me to meet a refugee named Umm Haze, who invited me into her makeshift home and offered me a cup of sweet tea. She asked me not to use her real name, but told me that it's a common honorific for women in her culture to be identified as the mother of her eldest son. 'Umm' means 'mother' and 'Haze' is her 14-year-old son's name.

Umm Haze has lived in Za'atari for almost six years, arriving pregnant with her youngest child, who is the same age as my son, Theo. The playful little girl with big brown eyes knows no life other than living in a single room in a glorified shipping container with her five siblings. Although we shared no common language, culture or circumstances, Umm Haze and I recognised our bond as mothers worried for the future of our kids. She described how her older children still have nightmares about the bombings and her deep regret that Haze has just dropped out of the UNHCR school in order to pick vegetables and earn a few extra dinars for the family.

My own worries about how Jules and I were going to afford the repairs to our ageing sewerage system soon felt trifling as the single mother explained that despite having to rely on food vouchers and despite her leaky tin roof, camp life was still better than the alternative – going back to a country devastated by war. 'Even if the war ended, I don't have a home to go back to,' she said.

Earlier this year, Dara'a was reduced to rubble by air strikes and artillery fire.[4] When I asked Umm Haze how she finds time for her own needs, her resolve faltered. 'I think that Allah is keeping me just for the sake of these children. I'm tired. I swear to Allah that I am tired,' she said through tears.

Even if Umm Haze were able to find a moment to herself to seek emotional support, there's only one psychiatrist available for the camp of 80 000 people. Although aid agencies and refugee organisations are contributing much-needed food, water, housing, clothing, education and social programs, the troubling reality is that most refugees are just like Umm Haze: people who have been uprooted by war, famine and persecution; people who have faced unimaginable trauma and who, marooned in no man's land, have no capacity to plan for a future even if they wanted to. These people, in the worst of the worst of circumstances, may never have access to *any* kind of mental health service, let alone interventions that are backed by evidence.[5]

Later that night, back in the comfort of my hotel room in Amman, I wept for the cruelty of a senseless conflict that I could not stop. I wept for the untended emotional scars of my fellow human beings and my impotence and uselessness in being able to do anything about the inevitable consequences of trauma on future generations. Although billions of dollars have been spent combatting epidemics such as Ebola and AIDS, the mental health of refugees is not an international priority. When the problem is this vast and this complicated, how could mindfulness possibly help?

Across the border in Israel, I found a team of researchers from the University of Haifa asking the very same question.

Inhumanity

RIP angel

I wonder what she called you, little one?

Your precious Mama …

Maybe she called you Berhan? … my light

Or did she call you Haben? … my pride

She may have called you Qisanet … after rest she yearned

Or were you Awet? … Victory …

Tell me little one did she name you after her hope?

Or her aspirations … her dreams?

Did she call you Amen as end to her prayers?

Did she name you after the saints your Grandma prayed to?

Or were you named after the brother she lost in prison?

Maybe after her father long gone?

Did she name you … Sinai … after the desert she crossed?

Or Eritrea … the land she reluctantly left …?

Perhaps she named you for the land you were to inherit?
Tell me little one what did your precious Mama call you?
For I can't bear you being called number 92 ...

by Selam Kidane, 6 October 2013[6]

They started arriving in Israel en masse in the mid-2000s: tens of thousands of men, women and children escaping a brutal dictatorship in Eritrea and a deadly civil war in Sudan. They had no choice. It was leave or face violent attacks, sexual assault, military conscription, enslavement, religious persecution, systemic torture, prison camps and famine.[7]

They paid smugglers and fled in a wave across the Egyptian Sinai desert. Bedouin tribesmen saw a lucrative opportunity and an extortion industry soon flourished as lawless criminal gangs established mass torture camps. The helpless East African hostages were chained, beaten, raped, electrocuted and burned, as their relatives listened on the other end of a phone line until they were able to scrounge ransom money. In what must be one of the most underreported travesties in recent history, it's estimated that 25000 to 30000 people were tortured in those desert camps. Thousands more died and lie in unmarked graves.[8–13]

In late 2012, the Israeli government completed a fence along its border with Egypt which drastically reduced the number of asylum seekers opting for that particular route. The action also put the Bedouin torturers out of business, at least in the Sinai.[14] Nevertheless, 40000 escapees had already made it past the gunfire of Egyptian soldiers, over the Gulf of Suez, through Israeli border patrols, and are now living in a multicultural melting pot in South Tel Aviv.

According to research conducted by psychologist and professor Amit Bernstein and his team at the Observing Minds Lab at the University of Haifa, Eritrean and Sudanese asylum seekers in Israel are among the most traumatised people on earth. 'Up to 70 or 80 per cent have either survived torture or witnessed torture and half of the population has either suffered or witnessed sexual assault. Those are extraordinarily high numbers. In some of our samples – these are community samples, not treatment seekers – we're talking about rates of post-traumatic stress disorder symptoms, elevated symptoms, of between 55 to 80 per cent.'

Amit and his team initially set out to research what makes refugees resilient after suffering unspeakable trauma, but when they learned of the depth of the invisible mental scars of the East African runaways in Israel, they had no choice but to change course. 'The consequences in their lives now are that they have nightmares and hyper-arousal, fear, anxiety and depression, not to mention the consequences for generations on their children, on their children's children, in terms of intergenerational transmission of that kind of damage to human psyches and human lives ... so yeah, we have to act now.'

Although there's a limited body of experimental clinical research on refugee mental health, with the help of a small research grant Amit's team spent months scouring scientific journals looking for clues as to what constitutes an effective trauma intervention. Borrowing elements from programs such as Mindfulness Based Stress Reduction (MBSR) and Cognitive Behaviour Therapy (CBT), they adapted and developed a nine-week program which they've called Mindfulness Based Trauma Recovery for Refugees (MBTR-R). Their hope is to now put it to the test in all kinds of refugee settings – from camps, to cities and post-resettlement communities in new host countries.

Although they've taken care to make their program trauma-sensitive and culturally relevant (for example, there are no separate words for stress, depression and anxiety in Tigrinya, the language spoken in Eritrea), I nevertheless remained unconvinced. After all, it's not just historical trauma that asylum seekers are dealing with. In Israel, for instance, despite it being a country founded by forcibly displaced Jews, many nationals want them out. East African migrants have been classified as 'infiltrators' by the Israeli government and deportation is a daily threat.

In the face of all this, when people are psychologically bleeding out on the inside, I asked Amit what made him think that mindfulness could be anything more than a bandaid solution. How could it possibly meet the emotional needs of an East African in Israel or any other traumatised refugee? 'That's a fair question,' he replied. 'And here I think we need to balance what might be the most effective intensive, multi-systemic kind of intervention and reality; like, what is feasible?'

Amit explained that his team's challenge was to identify approaches that are realistic and pragmatic. They asked themselves questions such as: What can have the greatest reach? What can be delivered to groups? What can be delivered by para-professionals? 'You can't have a psychiatrist, one or two or three or even 20 treating 150 000 refugees in a refugee camp,' he said. The intervention would also have to be relatively simple, affordable and, importantly, because the world is such a diverse place, minimally mediated. 'That is, more experience and less talk. Talk therapy as a cure-all for refugee mental health is never going to work.' With that in mind, Amit concluded that mindfulness interventions, although not a panacea, do meet each and every one of his criteria.

CASE STUDY #3 – PART 1

Mogos Kidane Tewelde
Eritrean Asylum Seeker

[Edited transcript]

Mogos: My name is Mogos and I was born in Dekemhare, Eritrea. I left in 2009.

The political situation in Eritrea is one party and one president almost for 28 years. There are no elections. There is no free movement. There is no free press. There is no free speech.

My mother was a housewife and my father was a soldier. They have eight children. How do you think they could manage with such a limited amount of money?

Your future is very dark because by the age of 18 you are like their property and they make you join the military to prepare to fight with Ethiopia. They tell you what to do, where to go and what not to do. You are not safe.

Me: So you left?

Mogos: Before the military called, I left. I went to Ethiopia, but I was caught and put in a refugee camp where the situation was very difficult. It was just like a prison. Illegally, we paid some smugglers to get us out to Sudan. But I had to leave after ten days, because it was not safe. How can I say it? There were some ... kidnappers ... they call your parents and make you pay a lot of money.

So we paid some more smugglers to take us through the Egyptian desert at night. There were almost 20 people in the Toyota pick-up. They treat you very badly. You can say that they are not human at all.

They only care about the money. It's not that they care about you. For example, in the desert, you don't have water. They put petrol into the water so you cannot drink.

And then we had to cross the Gulf of Suez in a very small boat with a lot of people. Almost 40 or 50 people or something like that. But there was a storm. The waves were very big. The boat was full of water. I saw with my own eyes that the captain of the boat was very scared. He was trembling. I thought if he spends his life at sea and he's scared, then this means death. It was terrible. Everyone was screaming, crying, vomiting.

From there after almost 10 hours, we reached the border of Israel. Then the Israeli soldiers caught us and took us to camps. After three weeks they brought us on the bus to Levinsky Park in South Tel Aviv and I start to live here in Israel.

Me: Do you regret making the journey?

Mogos: It is a crazy decision to give your life to someone you don't know, but when you are in that situation it is very stressful. You have no option and then you choose the very

tough decision to die or to win. I cannot say I regret it, but it is
the price I needed to pay to reach here.

I try to forget most of it because it's a very bad memory.
But sometimes, when I think about the border and the Gulf of
Suez, I remember it.

The University of Haifa team are in the midst of a
randomised controlled clinical trial in South Tel Aviv with
four intervention groups of East African asylum seekers: two
groups of men and two groups of women. 'The bottom line is
we don't think we're *curing* PTSD by delivering a mindfulness-
based intervention,' Amit said, 'but they're all recovering from
trauma and we have reason to think that if we can teach them
to engage in more mindful ways of being with their internal
life, with their memories, with the emotional pain and the
struggles in their lives, with their instability, uncertainty and
unpredictability, then perhaps they will be more likely to be
able to enjoy the *moments* in their lives that may be pleasant or
positive. They may be more likely to have some choice about
how they engage with themselves or with others as opposed
to being more driven from a place of fear, or automaticity, or
aversion, and so on.'

After our interview, I arranged to meet Amit in the heart
of South Tel Aviv. By day, it's a multicultural industrial hub.
By night, it's a hotspot for prostitution and drug dealing.
Although I felt safe accompanied by my cinematographer and
the University of Haifa team, this is not the kind of place I
would want to be on my own once the sun went down.

We met out the front of a dilapidated building on a busy main street. After chains and a padlock had been removed from an iron gate at the entrance, we made our way up a dank stairwell to the fourth floor. After rounding a corner, I found myself in what felt like a safe haven, a place called Kuchinate (which means 'crochet' in Tigrinya), the headquarters of an NGO on a mission to help Eritrean women earn a living making eco-friendly cloth baskets and homewares.

In the bright, welcoming studio, surrounded by shelves of colourful crocheted baskets, I found a dozen East African men sitting on flamboyant fabric-covered sofas ... meditating. They were being guided in a 'Loving-Kindness Meditation' by Ron Elon, Israel's equivalent of my meditation teacher, Patrick Kearney.

CASE STUDY #3 – PART 2

Mogos Kidane Tewelde
Eritrean Asylum Seeker
[Edited transcript]

Mogos: We refugees face a lot of problems, especially with the [risk of] deportation. It is the mind that makes me crazy and depressed. Because all the time, think think think, I'm addicted to it. I don't know how to stop. When I stop, I get peace. When I don't know how to stop, I get crazy or I get depressed.

Me: What did they teach you to do in the mindfulness course?

Mogos: The course explained the habits of the mind, how to stop it and how to get back to yourself. After you meditate you become a new person. You start to ask yourself, is that me, I'm just walking on the streets, I have no problems? And then after so many hours you get back to where you have been. For a few brief minutes, you become someone very new.

Me: Is it difficult for you?

Mogos: In the beginning it was very difficult because the mind wants to think and you don't want to think while you are meditating. But after a while you learn how to not think and it's very joyous. You get peace and you start to get very clear after you meditate.

Me: When I heard they were doing meditation with refugees who had been through horrible experiences, my first thought was that it's too much, it's too difficult. The last thing that refugees want to do is think. Do you think meditation is good for refugees?

Mogos: It's very good for refugees. But only if they get it in detail. So when you meditate, it's a state of getting the mind to rest and then after the mind rests you can bring a very clear or very clean state of thinking. The refugees here need it. I hope it will be distributed to all of the people and become part of the refugee system.

Me: This is incredible because you've got so many very big worries, finding time to meditate is almost a luxury.

Mogos: It's like a medicine for me. It might be a luxury for you, but it's a medicine for me.

For a Lifetime

The initial findings from what the team are calling 'Moments of Refuge' look promising. 'Some of the feedback from the participants so far has been pretty amazing,' said Amit. 'People, men and women, saying things like "I relate to my experience in a totally new way" and "I didn't know I was on autopilot". We had even one woman say that she used to struggle with anger and explosiveness at home and hit her children out of rage, and in the middle of the intervention she just stopped. That's it. And the preliminary data shows that compared to controls, we're seeing an almost 50 per cent drop in stress- and trauma-related symptoms after nine weeks of mindfulness.'

It will be another six months before the research team has final results, but despite the encouraging signs, my glimpse into the true potential for programs like MBTR-R didn't come from my conversations with Amit or even Mogos. Rather, my moment of conviction came later, during an unexpected conversation with Dawit Habtai, the program's cultural liaison and translator who quietly took me aside after we'd shared a delicious traditional Eritrean meal prepared by some of the women working at Kuchinate.

With Amit translating, Dawit told me that he'd been drafted as a young boy into the Eritrean army. After being wounded and attempting an escape, he was captured and tortured for five years before finally making the perilous journey to Israel.[15] He now works taking crisis support calls at the only mental health clinic available for his fellow African asylum seekers, which means that he's not only dealing with the demons of his own past and his own uncertain future, but he's also taking on the mental load of others. 'In the place I work, there is nothing I haven't heard,' he said. 'There are people in this world too cruel to even call people. I hear about violence, about physical abuse, sexual abuse, about watching their friends get shot at the border.'

Dawit made a point of sharing his story with me to explain that if someone offered him either 10 000 Israeli shekels or mindfulness training, he'd take the mindfulness training. It's the only time anyone has ever taught him how he can heal himself. 'I don't want someone to come and donate money. I don't want handouts. I want them to teach me how to solve my own problems. And that's what most asylum seekers want, someone to give them a tool,' he explained, before turning to Amit and telling him that participating in the mindfulness program is the best thing that has happened to him. 'I will never forget anyone who accompanied me to this point.'

Amit was moved to tears. He had no idea that the usually stoic and reserved former child solider felt that way. 'I don't want to get too excited because we have to wait until we've finished the randomised controlled clinical trial, but we're seeing virtually no adverse responses, so it seems that this program is indeed safe and effective for even the most traumatised people on the planet. It's pretty amazing.'

Although it's going to take a lot more than a single nine-week program to address the unmet psychological needs of the world's forcibly displaced people, in the gaping absence of other evidence-informed solutions, my visit to Amit's mobile lab in the urban slums of South Tel Aviv left me in no doubt that programs like his are a great start.

As I boarded the plane bound for the sanctuary of my own peaceful country, towards my husband and kids and our perfectly imperfect house on Sydney's sparkling northern beaches, the hopelessness I felt after my visit to Za'atari was replaced by something new: a sense of purpose. An old expression kept turning over in my mind: *Give a man a fish and he will be hungry tomorrow. Teach him how to fish and he'll be fed for a lifetime.*

CHAPTER TEN

The Happiness of Pursuit

'What does the story mean, then?'

'It means what you want it to mean,' Hoid said. 'The purpose of a storyteller is not to tell you how to think, but to give you questions to think upon. Too often, we forget that.'

– From Brandon Sanderson's novel
The Way of the Kings[1]

Results

I've always loved the idea of a 'MacGuffin', a storytelling concept popularised by the late, great pioneer of the thriller genre, Alfred Hitchcock. Whether it's the 'One Ring', the 'Philosopher's Stone', or the 'Holy Grail', my favourite stories are propelled by the search for an object, location, person, or deeply desired goal.

Now that I'm at the end of this experiment I realise that, from the start, I was unwittingly in search of my own MacGuffin:

a black and white, yes or no, scientific answer as to whether daily mindfulness training could be a missing link in our global mental health crisis. I was looking for the mental equivalent of a jog around the block, or eating at least five servings of fresh fruit and vegetables each day; something that anyone could do – regardless of education, location, culture or circumstance – to protect, nurture and nourish the mind.

Like in all good stories, my MacGuffin became a sidebar to the real narrative that unfolded. In the same way that Harry Potter's quest ended up being about identity, friendship and family, and Frodo Baggins learned about courage, selflessness and loyalty, I too have been transformed in unexpected and unintended ways. And after more than 100 scientific tests, 365 experiment days, and 453 hours of meditation, I now have the results.

1. Brain Activity

Using an electroencephalogram (EEG), Dr Neil Bailey from the Alfred Psychiatry Research Centre at Monash University measured electrical activity in my brain. He was especially interested to know if my training reflected what he'd found in a randomised controlled trial involving 70 people, in which 34 experienced meditators had better attention and working memory during certain tasks.[2] Neil's experienced meditators had been training on average about 5.5 hours per week for eight years; he wanted to see if my training was nudging me in the same direction.

With the help of PhD candidate Jonathan Davies from the

University of Sydney, on seven occasions (two before I started meditating to establish a reliable baseline and five subsequent times throughout my mindful year) the researchers attached 64 electrodes to my scalp and then gave me the same lab challenges that Neil had given to his study participants. The tasks involved doing things such as trying not to react to emotive faces, and remembering specific letters in a sequence that were momentarily flashed on a screen. Neil also tested my resting state and meditating states during each session.

The results showed that although there were clear differences in my brain activity when I was resting and when I was meditating, there was huge variability in my overall brain signals from scan to scan. Neil concluded that because my brain activity was so wildly different day to day, there wasn't a clear signal coming through. Even if my attention and working memory were improving, the EEG-generated brain waves wouldn't show it. This is why scientists need so many people to participate in their studies in order to get meaningful results.

'So you're saying an EEG can't actually capture an overall feeling of wellbeing and inner peace in one person?' I asked him over the phone.

'Maybe it can, but we don't know what that looks like yet,' he said.

When I look back on my notes from each of my EEG scans, Neil's results make sense. Two of the scans required waking up at 5.00 a.m. to catch flights to Melbourne, another scan was done while I had a raging headache and was coming down with the flu. I also found the attention tasks far more difficult on days when Jules was there filming me for the documentary.

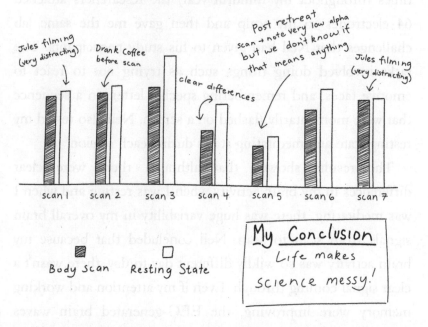

EEG RESULTS
ALPHA ACTIVITY

Jules filming (very distracting)

Drank Coffee before scan

Post retreat scan → note very low alpha but we don't know if that means anything

clear differences

Jules filming (very distracting)

scan 1   scan 2   scan 3   scan 4   scan 5   scan 6   scan 7

■ Body Scan   ☐ Resting State

My Conclusion
Life makes science messy!

My conclusion? You just can't meditate away the impact of real-life interference like sleep deprivation, the flu, or having a camera lens filming 10 centimetres in front of your face. Life makes science messy.

2. Brain Structure and Connectivity

My brain did change throughout my year of living mindfully, though. Professor Nicolas Cherbuin used magnetic resonance imaging (MRI) and functional magnetic resonance imaging (fMRI) to track its structure and function, and his scans showed structural changes in a number of regions. While most brains start shrinking when we reach our early 20s, four areas in my brain that relate to self-awareness, memory and dealing with emotions did the opposite, and grew.

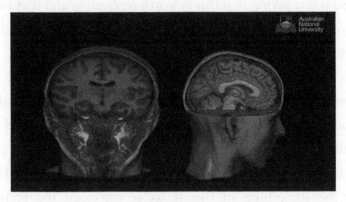

My brain

'When you look at your left hippocampus, for example, it's increasing at a higher rate than we thought it would decrease,' said Nic. Aside from structural changes, he also found surprising changes in connectivity between brain regions. 'I told you at the beginning that it was unlikely we would be able to see changes in your brain in this period of time. I wasn't certain we could detect anything useful to interpret, let alone attribute it to meditative practice.' When the fMRI demonstrated a clear difference between my brain at resting state and meditation state, Nic was willing to add it to the overall story and attribute the changes to daily mindfulness practice, rather than me being some kind of freak of nature.

He explained that my larger hippocampus was significant because smaller hippocampal brain regions are associated with mental illnesses such as depression and cognitive diseases such as Alzheimer's. The idea that meditation could be like a brain fitness workout was intriguing. 'This study has good methodology and there is no reason why we couldn't do it in larger number of people,' Nic said.

'So you're saying that this is worth replicating and that I need to go and recruit you another 20 people willing to meditate every day for a year?' I asked.

'It's absolutely something that needs to be done,' he said before turning the line of questioning around on me, asking about my retreat experience, and pondering how he could find the time to add meditation to his own To Do list.

I turned to Jules, who was filming our conversation. 'There must be something in this if we've intrigued the sceptical neuroscientist enough to consider giving it a try!'

3. Physical Health

Scientists are currently debating whether mindfulness could have effects throughout our body and impact our physical health. And the answer is ... yes, absolutely. But when, where, why and how: that's where it gets interesting.

Although part of me hoped I'd be cured of my autoimmune disease, my medical results showed that I still have positive antinuclear antibodies (ANA) and extractable nuclear antigens (ENA) in my blood. Despite being symptom free after I returned from the retreat, after spending time in the Middle East, and again in the final push as we wrapped up filming, I experienced two more brief pain flare-ups. But the pain didn't bother me. No sleepless nights. No freaking out that my health was in tatters and no fretting about my future. Each episode lasted less than a week and I didn't need to take any medication.

At my last check-up Dr Anna Finniss, my rheumatologist, said, 'The symptoms you've described – that delayed onset muscle soreness, the feeling that you've been to the gym when you haven't – are typical of fibromyalgia. It's brilliant that you've been able to improve that. At the moment it's mild, and when I test the numbers of antibodies you're making, they're at the low end ... Your symptoms guide me on what pathology is occurring and I'm really happy from my assessment today and from your blood tests that you're not manifesting any autoimmune phenomena. I would continue doing what you're doing.'

To further explore my mind–body connection, I engaged Stratech Scientific, a private laboratory which does analysis for researchers at numerous Australian universities. On the instructions of Stratech's General Manager, Mark Longster, once a month, five times a day, I provided saliva samples to track a series of markers associated with my immune function. This occurred when I was at home with the kids, had just been travelling, feeling well or feeling sick.

C-Reactive Protein Data

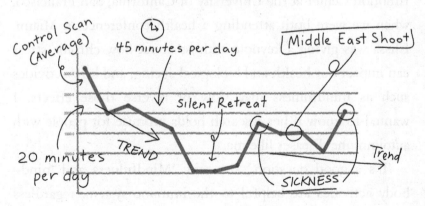

Stratech also analysed levels of the stress hormone cortisol in both my hair and saliva, and uncovered an unexpected anomaly. 'If your cortisol levels were any lower throughout the year, including when we took the control samples at the start, you'd probably be dead,' said Mark over the phone. While you might think that low levels of cortisol would be a good thing, in this circumstance it was perplexing. I'd expected that my stress markers would be off the chart before I began meditating and then perhaps spike again because of my international travel.

Early on in this experiment I was intrigued by Associate Professor Willoughby Britton's 'Variety of Contemplative Experiences' study which found that people who had trouble meditating also reported a wide variety of *interpretations* of those experiences, feeling everything from neutral curiosity, to bliss and joy, to fear and terror. I made a note that there may be something more to the idea that *how* I interpret or perceive things has repercussions in my body and overall health.

Shortly after meeting Willoughby, I spoke with Professor Elissa Epel, the Director of the Aging, Metabolism and Emotion Center at the University of California, San Francisco, when we were both attending a health conference in Miami. Elissa was giving a keynote address about how chronic stress can impact our health and biological ageing, and how activities such as mindfulness may slow or reverse those effects. I wanted to know if her research holds promise for people with autoimmune diseases like me.

'It's a good question,' she said. 'Mindfulness and mind–body activities are helpful to the immune system, regardless of whether it's overactive or under-active. We think that while genetics play a huge role, when you want to know who's living well to age 100, we think lifestyle plays a tremendous role and it's the interaction between lifestyle and experience with genetics. It's not about one or the other.'

I checked my notes to see if there was anything that could explain my consistently low cortisol readings. 'In general, in stress research, it has been found that exposure to a situation doesn't really determine mental health, let's say stress or depression, as much as how someone interprets the situation,' Elissa said. 'What actually happens to people is important, but if I were to put my money on one, I would say it's the psychological response to situations, not just whether a situation exists or not.'

Elissa was referring to research from the 1960s and 1970s when American physiologist John Wayne Mason found that our perception of a stressful event was critical to how our body responded to it.[3] Whereas one person may be terrified at the thought of public speaking, another might see it as an exciting challenge. Likewise, a divorce could be a stressor for one person but a major release of stress for another. Recent research has also shown that our performance and biology can respond according to a pre-primed 'threat' or 'challenge' mindset.[4]

This is why Elissa thinks mindfulness holds promise for reducing the impact that chronic stress has on our health, even more so than other relaxation activities. 'Mindfulness has this other layer of change because it teaches us how to understand and know our mind more intimately, so that when we have irrational, negative or self-critical thoughts, we can catch them and find the humour in them and laugh at them; or at least let them go instead of grabbing onto them and believing them.'

Maybe the haphazard mindfulness training I'd done prior to my year of living mindfully gave me more of a stress buffer than I'd realised? Or could it be that having a supportive husband meant that what I thought were stressful circumstances weren't affecting me physiologically? Could these reasons explain my low levels of cortisol?

In my search for clarity, I went back over my journal entries at the time the control samples were taken. My diarised stress levels were off the chart: I was anxious about tensions in my extended family, I had insomnia one or two nights a week and Isaac, our second baby, had just turned one. Even with my husband's support, I was struggling to keep up and adjust to life as a working mother of two. There were some days that I didn't have time to bathe, let alone find 'me' time.

Something still wasn't adding up.

It took further digging and the help of my GP to reveal the answer. It turned out I was anaemic. Iron deficiency was messing with my cortisol production.[5] Before this revelation, I'd put my fatigue down to being sleep deprived and having too much on my plate, but iron is the most common nutritional deficiency in the developed world and affects around one in three women of reproductive age.[6]

Being low in cortisol is a concern. Although it is best known for its role in our body's fight-or-flight stress response, it's also important in metabolism, our immune response, our circadian rhythm and for restoring balance after a stress response. Over the next few months I'll continue taking iron supplements prescribed by my GP and I'll also experiment with my diet until I get things back in balance.

I would have liked my health results to tell a neat, linear story and to clearly and biologically demonstrate one way or another how mindfulness 'works'. But I now understand why people like Nicholas Van Dam, the lead author of the 'Mind the Hype' paper, recommended asking questions when someone claims that a new intervention will work 100 per cent of the time for 100 per cent of people. He also warned me that the results will only ever serve as an interesting case study and won't say much about the effects of daily mindfulness meditation on anyone else, in different circumstances. And he's right. I'm increasingly sounding just like the authors of the hundreds of scientific papers I've picked apart in the last year, the ones that always seem to conclude, 'Yada yada yada, promising, but more research is needed'.

4. Cellular Health

When I conceived this experiment, I was fascinated by research demonstrating that mindfulness meditation is also associated with good health at a cellular level. In 2009, the Australian-born molecular biologist Elizabeth (Liz) Blackburn shared the Nobel Prize for Medicine for discovering 'telomeres', which are cap-like structures at the ends of chromosomes, a bit like the little protective plastic ends of shoelaces, that shorten as we age.[7] The shorter my telomeres, the more chance there is that my health will fray and I'll die at an earlier age.

In 2004, Liz and Elissa collaborated on a small but seminal study which compared the telomeres of two groups of mothers. One group were carers of disabled children, the other had healthy kids. 'Parenting is stressful, period, but if you have a child with a chronic condition, this just adds layers and layers of unease and worry, tension, vigilance, and you feel alone, too,' Elissa explained.

Although they expected that the women looking after disabled children would have older telomeres, there was no difference between the two groups. The revelation came when they looked at the women's levels of perceived stress. Regardless of whether they had disabled kids or not, the mothers who *felt* they had a lot of stress in their lives had a greater rate of cellular ageing. In fact, women who perceived themselves to have high stress had aged up to 17 additional years, compared with the low-stress group.[8]

Since then, meta-analysis has found that the more people meditate, the longer their telomeres.[9] Liz and Elissa have developed a theory that mindfulness may have beneficial effects on telomere length by reducing stress perception and increasing positive states of mind, which in turn have beneficial effects on biological pathways that promote telomere maintenance.[10] 'One of the cardinal features of mindfulness training is that it helps people become aware of their stress response. So rather than that automatic reaction, they're able to notice when they start to react and then to have a more of a reflective response,' Elissa explained.

Knowing that mindfulness training had affected my own stress perception, I was keen to find out if this had in turn affected my cellular age. I enlisted the help of a local lab and Associate Professor Hilda Pickett, who's the head of the

Telomere Length Regulation Unit at the University of Sydney's Children's Medical Research Institute. Hilda and her team extracted and measured my telomeres from 14 blood samples, two before I began meditating and 12 throughout my mindful year. The analysis showed that my telomeres may have grown, which is great news because having longer telomeres means that I'm less likely to succumb to diseases such as heart disease, diabetes, or cancer. But although it's tempting to hype this up, Hilda used three different telomere measuring techniques and they each showed different results.

'Am I right in thinking that it's not necessarily that there isn't an effect, but that we might not be able to measure one?' I asked her.

'What you're going to see with telomere length is going to be very, *very* subtle, and what this analysis actually shows is that there's a lot of variability in the techniques,' she said. 'Even just the error between the technical replicates of the samples is higher than the differences that you would expect to actually see in telomere length.'

Once again, this is why scientists like Liz, Elissa and Hilda rely on large sample sizes in their research. The more participants, the better. This doesn't take away from the intriguing research on large groups of people, but while the experts are refining their tools, it's difficult to study an individual's cellular health, let alone how mindfulness may affect it. I'm now more wary than ever of internet ads offering products to make my cells younger in six months and measure my age in 'TeloYears'.

'Those supplements might actually be accelerating cancer instead of preventing it,' Elissa said.

Elissa isn't a total sceptic, though. She suspects that all the stress reduction and emotion regulating that long-term meditators practise can result in their genes expressing differently.[11] Although we often think of our genes as being a fixed and unchangeable blueprint of who we are, our physical environment and social experiences can silence or turbo-charge the way genes code themselves.[12,13] In other words, genes have a 'volume control' that can be turned up and down and this explains why identical twins who have the same genetic blueprint can differ in their inherited diseases.[14]

In 2014, Richie Davidson and his team at the Center for Healthy Minds at the University of Wisconsin-Madison found that genes involved in creating inflammation got 'turned down' in 19 experienced meditators who attended a day of intensive meditation, but not in a control group of 21 non-meditators.[15]

I asked Richie about this promising pilot study when I met him in New York. 'Some people thought we were absolutely crazy to even think that we could see a change so rapidly. But we went ahead and did the experiment and we were able to see a change, and it was specifically for genes that had been implicated in inflammation. And that has important health implications, because we know that inflammatory processes are at the root of many chronic illnesses; cardiovascular disease, arthritis, asthma. If meditation can reduce inflammation, that's a really important finding.'

I couldn't hide my enthusiasm. 'It's early days, obviously, but that's extremely compelling for me as someone with an autoimmune disease,' I said.

'I agree, and it also helps us to better understand how the changes in the brain may be linked to changes in the body and to uncover the mechanisms that underlie the association between wellbeing and physical health, because people who report higher levels of wellbeing on average tend to be physically healthier. It's not all the time, it's not everyone, but on average that's true.'

The idea that my life experiences can reach into my DNA and change how my genes behave had me captivated.[16] For my own mindful experiment I recruited the help of Professor Marc Wilkins, the Director of the Ramaciotti Centre for Genomics at the University of New South Wales, who recruited the Molecular Genetic Team at the Garvan Institute of Medical Research. Led by Marc, a team of scientists across two campuses extracted my genetic information from 14 samples (including two controls) and turned them into microarrays from which they then analysed the expression of more than 17 000 genes throughout the year.

'There was something which did come up,' Marc said as he talked me through the final results in a UNSW teaching lab. Projected onto a huge teaching screen was a graph showing clear changes in a gene called PLA2G4A (Phospholipase A2 group IVA). 'This [gene] generates a very potent activator of inflammation. We're seeing a master regulator of inflammatory processes which is showing this greatest change throughout your mindfulness process.'

'That big dip there,' I clarified, looking at a cliff-like fall in the expression of my PLA2G4A gene. 'That's the first sample we took after I did the silent retreat. And that's showing that that gene is effectively switching off?'

EXPRESSION OF PLA2G4A GENE

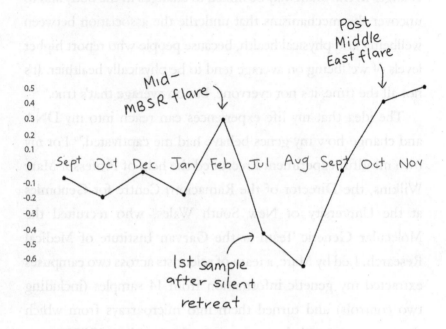

'That's right: it's being turned down; what we call being "down regulated",' said Marc.

The expression of my PLA2G4A gene tracks uncannily close to my experience of my autoimmune symptoms over the last year. Unfortunately, I'll never really know if the meditation training I did on the retreat led to the gene being 'turned down'. After all, for 10 days, in that natural bushland setting, I was also eating a healthy vegetarian diet, taking lots of walks in nature, getting plenty of kid-free sleep, and having a holiday from my inbox and To Do list. Nevertheless, as someone with an incurable autoimmune disease, who's been led to believe that my illness is caused by inherited bad genetic luck, it's electrifying to contemplate the idea that the genes associated with the inflammation in my body might be turned up and down depending on how I live my life.

'You're the world-leading scientist on gene expression and regulation; is this as interesting to you as it is to me?' I asked Marc.

'If I was going to do another experiment, I'd say, well, look, let's keep a careful eye on this gene because it *did* show some change. The change isn't what we call statistically significant because it's a study of one, but I think there's an interesting trend there.'

5. Mental Health

Having spent more than $30 000 on this experiment, I've come to the realisation that of all the multitudes of scientific markers, there is now actually only one measurement that matters — how I *feel*. Ironically, I filled in the 100-question World Health Organisation's Quality of Life assessment (WHOQOL-100) when I was establishing the experiment protocols, but I didn't take it seriously as I thought my subjective experience was of little importance compared to hard data and objective results.

After filling in the questionnaire again, I got in touch with Kimina Lyall, a Doctor of Psychology (clinical) candidate at Deakin University, who has a special interest in mindfulness and subjective wellbeing. Although I'd completed a slightly different questionnaire to the one preferred by Kimina's team, she agreed to study up on the WHO measure and analyse my subjective wellbeing data. Before telling me what she found, she said, 'If your subjective experience of your life is that daily mindfulness is good for you, do you need someone else to tell you?'

'No, I guess I don't,' I replied, knowing that I would keep meditating no matter what the results were.

'That's the point of subjective wellbeing research; in fact, you could argue that it's the only valid tool.'

Kimina's doctorate supervisor, Robert (Bob) Cummins, is a legend in wellbeing research. Bob has surveyed tens of thousands of people over almost 20 years and found that the population average for subjective wellbeing sits around 75 percentage points, give or take a few. That is, most of us score 75.02 out of 100 in questionnaires about wellbeing and quality of life.[17]

Bob's theory of 'Subjective Wellbeing Homeostasis' has some similarities with a concept in social psychology known as the 'Hedonic Treadmill'. Like all social science, there's nuance, but generally the evidence suggests that despite the highs and lows we may experience in our lives, most of us have a happiness baseline to which we are destined to return.[18] The Hedonic Treadmill is why people who win the lottery ultimately end up no happier, or how people who have debilitating accidents often emotionally bounce back.[19] In fact, a growing body of research done with identical and fraternal twins suggests that how happy you'll be is likely to be 35 to 50 per cent due to your genetic make-up.[20-24] Some researchers think this factor may even be as high as 80 per cent.[25]

According to Bob's theory, our homeostatic system

SUBJECTIVE WELLBEING HOMEOSTASIS THEORY

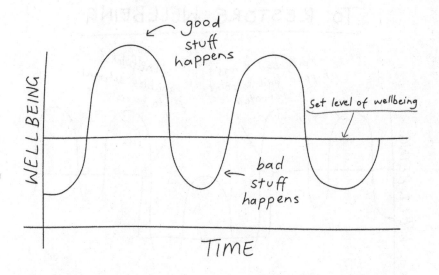

maintains our wellbeing set point within a range, allowing for minor variations from day to day, or even year to year.

Small disappointments or achievements are unlikely to nudge our subjective wellbeing outside of that range; however, when really bad things happen – say, we lose our job, go through a horrendous divorce, or a loved one dies – we can be knocked out of our set point range. If we're able to draw on external resources such as our finances and support networks to get us through, then we can find new behaviours and habits and get back to normal. If, however, the challenge is greater and more prolonged, or we experience multiple challenging events at the same time, we can go into 'homeostatic failure', aka depression.[26] Kimina's compelling (but as yet untested) theory is that mindfulness could be a tool to help people recover their natural homeostatic set point.

HOW MINDFULNESS MIGHT BE ABLE TO RESTORE WELLBEING

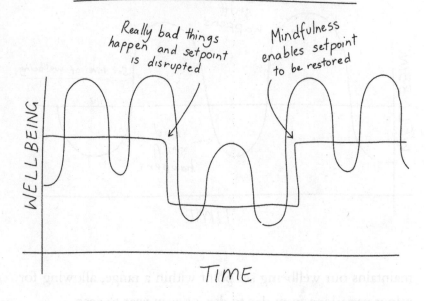

Really bad things happen and setpoint is disrupted

Mindfulness enables setpoint to be restored

WELLBEING

TIME

At the start of the experiment, Kimina's calculations revealed I was slightly below the average person's wellbeing set point, measuring 69.4 out of 100. By the end, after 365 days of meditation, an eight-week Mindfulness Based Stress Reduction course and a 10-day silent retreat, my subjective wellbeing improved to 93, which is well above average.

'So, like, almost 100 per cent happy?' I asked Kimina.

'Pretty much, yes. Another way to look at these two numbers is to say that you were kind of at the low end of your set point range at the beginning and now you're at the high end,' said Kimina, being careful to explain that I hadn't collected enough data at the start to accurately calculate my set point, so we can't know for sure whether or not I have gone from outside of my own set point range (i.e., homeostatic defeat) to within it (homeostatic control).

'So you've maybe bought yourself a bit of wiggle room to have those kind of life setbacks and have them not knock you out of your homeostatic range,' she hypothesised.

What I find interesting about this result is that before the experiment I was exercising regularly and eating a healthy, mostly junk-free diet. I lived in a peaceful, stable country, had meaningful work, healthy kids, a loving husband and good social support. I ticked all the boxes for what 'should' constitute a subjectively happy person. And yet I was still below average on the wellbeing scale. By the end of my mindful year, I still had all those things going for me, but when I added daily mindfulness meditation into the mix, my score improved markedly.

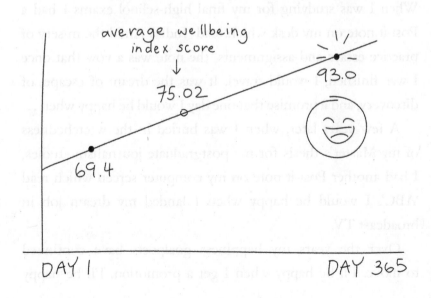

MY SUBJECTIVE WELLBEING RESULTS

average wellbeing index score

75.02

93.0

69.4

DAY 1   DAY 365

What I find even more interesting is that my score changed despite the fact I was still concerned about unwell family members, despite my experiences in the Middle East, despite the homesickness induced by international and domestic travel, despite my arthritic flare-ups, despite still dancing the impossible work–life twostep, and despite the financial pressure that accompanies making an independent feature film on a shoestring budget. Even with *all* this, at the end of my mindful year, I found a way of being that feels much like how I once felt as a young girl. It's as though my naturally ingrained sense of wellbeing has been restored.

Happy When ...

What is happiness? It's the moment before you need more happiness.

Don Draper, *Mad Men*[27]

When I was studying for my final high-school exams I had a Post-it note on my desk which read 'India'. Amid the misery of practice essays and assignments, the note was a vow that once I was finished, I would travel. It was the dream of escape, of discovery, and a promise that one day I would be happy when ...

A few years later, when I was buried in the wretchedness of my Master's thesis for my postgraduate journalism studies, I had another Post-it note on my computer screen which read 'ABC'. I would be happy when I landed my dream job in broadcast TV.

Over the years my happiness goalposts have continued to move. I'll be happy when I get a promotion. I'll be happy when I've saved a deposit for a house. I'll be happy when I'm married … when I'm a mother … when I've made my film … written my book … made another film … written another book … *meditated every day for a year* …

From an evolutionary psychologist's perspective, this eternal striving for satisfaction makes perfect sense. If my savannah-roaming Homo sapiens ancestors were completely satisfied after eating a meal, they would soon have died in a state of contented starvation. Being happily fed might have been a nice way to finish their own brief lives, but it would not have aided the bigger mission of procreation and raising kids who would in turn keep the gene pool alive. For this reason, instead of granting lasting satiation from a delicious meal, Mother Nature gave my forebears a kind of tug-of-war relationship to food. They ate, felt good, then after a while felt hungry and discontented, which motivated them to again find food.

From a behaviourist's perspective, this same perpetual discontent is driven by 'operant conditioning' or 'reinforcement learning' (that brain-based learning system we share with sea slugs) which means our behaviour is motivated by doing things that result in positive rather than negative outcomes.[28] In other words, we're all driven by seeking pleasure and avoiding suffering.

When the Rolling Stones sang 'I can't get no satisfaction' they were tapping into a fundamental principle in both behaviourism and evolutionary psychology. When I try and try, like Mick Jagger, an in-built, hardwired, survival-of-the-species motivational force steals my contentment and leaves dissatisfaction in its place. By virtue of Darwinian design happiness does not, and cannot, last.[29]

The slipperiness of my happiness and the inevitability of my wanting, craving, seeking, desiring, and bettering also happens to align with the cornerstone of Buddhist teaching – suffering and relief from suffering. Back in the day, Siddhārtha Gautama, the world's original mindfulness teacher, is said to have laid out the 'Four Noble Truths', a set of lessons that convey everything people need to know in their quest for inner peace. And the first Noble Truth? It's all about something he called *dukkha*.

According to Bhikkhu Bodhi, an American Theravada monk who is famous for his translations of the earliest Buddhist scriptures, *dukkha* is an ancient Pāli word which literally translates as 'suffering'. But *dukkha* means much more than just pain and misery. It refers to a basic dissatisfaction running through our lives. 'Sometimes this dissatisfaction erupts as sorrow, grief, disappointment, or despair; but usually it hovers at the edge of our awareness as a vague unlocalised sense that things are never quite perfect, never fully adequate to our expectations of what they should be,' Bodhi writes in his book *The Noble Eightfold Path: The Way to the End of Suffering*.[30]

Clichéd though it may be, the understanding that until now I've been fruitlessly chasing happiness rainbows is one of my biggest revelations.

Despite the boost in subjective wellbeing in my final results, I still don't think that meditation has made me any happier. Rather, I think mindfulness teaches me how to be *less unhappy*. I'm learning to turn towards my painful thoughts and feelings and to know that the bad times are just as much a part of this thing we call life as the good times. I'm learning to be *discomfortable* and, by doing so, I'm tapping into an ever-present undercurrent of inner wellbeing.

If Siddhārtha were around today, he might call this thing that I've been learning *equanimity*. Indeed, Buddhist texts define equanimity as a 'neutral feeling, a mental feeling which leans neither to gladness nor dejection and is manifested as peacefulness.'[31] Kimina and her team at Deakin might also say that this aligns with their research on the homeostatic set point. In their model, equanimity is akin to something they call Homeostatically Protected Mood (HPMood), and their research indicates that having a capacity to tap into this 'mildly pleasant, free-floating, and object-free mood state that underlies conscious experience' may be key to helping people get back to a healthy wellbeing set point after they've been knocked around.[32]

Researchers at Harvard, including Sara Lazar, who did the seminal brain scans on long-term meditators, are also thinking along the same lines. They recently published a paper proposing that equanimity, which they describe as an 'even-minded mental state or dispositional tendency toward all experiences or objects, regardless of their origin or their affective valence (pleasant, unpleasant, or neutral)' may be 'the most important psychological element in the improvement of wellbeing'.[33]

Perhaps it is equanimity that ABC news anchor Dan Harris, who turned to mindfulness after having a panic attack live on air in front of five million people, is talking about when he describes mindfulness as an ability to know what's happening in his head without getting carried away by it. Perhaps equanimity is what Vidyamala Burch, who bears incessant chronic pain from a horrific, incurable spinal injury, means when she says that mindfulness is not about finding a miracle cure, but rather about learning to live with her life, whatever arises. And perhaps it is equanimity that is helping Eritrean asylum seekers like Dawit Habtai and Mogos Kidane Tewelde. Perhaps their mindfulness training has given them the precious inner resource of equanimity which helps them bear the pain of their unimaginable suffering and ongoing uncertainty.

As I contemplated the end of this yearlong experiment, the slipperiness of my own satisfaction, and this newfound glimpse of inner calm and equilibrium, I also began paying attention to the by-products of my search. Wanting things to be better led me to do just one more practice essay before my high-school exams, to volunteer for just one more internship at university, to dig just a little deeper when I was a news reporter and to take the frightening leap of leaving mainstream journalism to become an independent filmmaker. My quest for lasting happiness also led me to marry Jules and to experience the bone-deep terror, tiredness, joy and delight of raising a family.

Whether I call it operant conditioning, Homeostatically Protected Mood, release from *dukkha*, or a quest for inner peace, my year of living mindfully has taught me that my time on this planet – the by-product of my pursuit for happiness, with all its stops and starts, ups and downs, hurdles and roundabouts – has been rather fantastic. Perhaps it's not so much happiness I should be pursuing but the pursuit of the pursuit of happiness, or, rather, the happiness of pursuit.

Likelihood that I'll be meditating daily 12 months from now? 100 per cent.

My Life of Living Mindfully

Day 982

Although I know I could use the results of my year of living mindfully to give this story a happily-ever-after fairytale ending, the truth is I don't wake up every morning in a permanent state of bliss. I'm still finding it difficult to put aside time to meditate. It's still easier to sit and watch TV in my rare moments of downtime rather than sit with my sometimes pleasant, but often uncomfortable, thoughts and feelings. But now, more than ever, my mindfulness practice has become an essential part of my daily life.

The world is a very different place to what it was when I began the experiment. I'm writing these words during a global medical emergency. Like around one-third of the world's population, I'm in isolation at home with my family, having made it home from North America just in time, after the film festival where I was premiering the feature documentary of this project was shut down, and right before the Australian borders were closed.

The spread of COVID-19 has necessitated the cancellation of sporting, religious, political and cultural events. Schools, universities and colleges have closed. The airline, tourism and hospitality industries have collapsed and, just a few short months since we first heard about a viral illness in China, with hundreds of thousands across the globe now dead, we are already in the midst of one of the largest global recessions in history.

Like everyone else, I feel concern for my dear ones. Although the majority of people infected experience only mild symptoms or none at all, I'm worried for my parents who are in their mid-60s, for my in-laws who are in their mid-70s, and for my two great-grandmothers who are 87 and 91 respectively.

With no vaccine in sight and no known effective antiviral medication yet developed, life is unlikely to be 'normal' again for a long, long time. In these uncharted waters, mindfulness is my map and people like Craig Hassed, my friend and mindfulness mentor from Monash University, are my compass.

Craig and I connected today over a video call. 'If this feels like a bit of a marathon, well it might be, but a marathon is one step at a time. If we think we've got 40 000 steps to get to the other end of this, we can feel overwhelmed. But if we realise that we're just taking one step at a time – in this moment it might be our conversation over Skype, in the next, it might just be a tea bag in a teacup, and in the next it might be having a bite to eat – mindfulness training can help us to direct our mind to the present and life becomes a lot more manageable.' He asked if I was still meditating daily and reminded me that the formal practice is really just training for mindfulness in my daily life; in the work I'm doing, in my relationship with Jules, in the way I'm guiding my kids through this, and how I'm supporting others whom I care about.

The rest of the world seems like a long way away as I try to keep my kids educated and entertained at home, and while Jules and I indefinitely reschedule more than 150 worldwide film screenings and pivot to an online release for our documentary that has been almost three years in the making. As I juggle and struggle with all this, my mindfulness training allows me to step back from my own problems, to take a particular vantage point, and to ponder my difficulties with discernment and, hopefully, wisdom.

While the pandemic health experts advise on the best containment strategies and necessary restrictions in order to save lives and reduce the impact of the virus on our already over-burdened healthcare systems, I can't help but turn my mind to the collateral damage. We were already losing the battle against chronic stress, pain, mental illness, addiction and rising suicide rates before all this began; what will months and potentially years of political instability, job losses, school closures and social isolation do to us? What will the long-term mental health effects be on the isolated, jobless and homeless? And their children?

We already know that past crises have led to growing mental health problems and spikes in suicide rates[1]. A review of studies investigating the psychological effects of quarantine published in *The Lancet* found that symptoms of post-traumatic stress disorder (PTSD), confusion and anger were common.[2]

Other studies have shown that substantial job displacement significantly increased mortality rates over time, possibly through stress and income shocks.[3]

When health economists, clinical psychologists and social researchers start finding their voice in this unfolding story, there's one thing I know for sure: the ultimate cost of this pandemic will not only be measured by the number of lives lost, or the number of businesses that failed, the levels of national debt, or the unemployment rates. It will be measured by things such as the number of healthcare workers who are diagnosed with PTSD, the number of people who take their own lives because they can't get a job, and the number of young people who emerge from isolation with new mental health problems and addictions to technology. All of these tolls will leave their mark on the mental health of a generation.

I keep thinking about the refugees I met in the Za'atari camp on the border of Syria and Jordan, and the African asylum seekers I met in South Tel Aviv. The emotional needs of these people, who have no income and no option to return home, will likely be forgotten as the funding capacities of charities dry up and the aid agendas of world leaders turn inwards. As it is, only a fraction of the millions of refugees worldwide receive any kind of mental health support, let alone interventions backed by evidence.

My hope is that the majority of people will have the external support and inner resources to make peace with the world's chaos and recover quickly. We know from research done after 9/11 that people have a remarkable capacity for resilience after trauma and adversity.[4] And while many governments are already doing their part to cushion the blow with tax cuts, stimulus packages and various financial safeguards, we're still in the opening paragraphs of this saga.

I began my mindful experiment at a time when the statistics on mental health were already tracking in all the wrong directions, and when 28 world-leading mental health experts had just publicly declared that *every* country in the world was facing and *failing* to tackle a host of mental health crises.[5] And while we don't yet know how many people will die from COVID-19, we do know that 264 million people suffer from depression and 800 000 people commit suicide globally each year. That's one person every 40 seconds.[6]

In this new era of worldwide political volatility, economic instability and environmental uncertainty, I'm convinced that we need evidence-based mindfulness programs more than ever. I'm not suggesting that mindfulness is a superior option than the best of psychopharmacology, psychiatry or psychology. But after what has now become a 982-day self-experiment, it's clear to me why mindfulness has earned its multi-decade record in modern medicine and healthcare, and why it's finding its way into education, business, social justice and politics. In all its simplicity and complexity, mindfulness is not an either-or proposition; it's an adjunct that complements the best of whatever else is available.

With the help of good mindfulness teachers, depressed people can step back from their despondency, people with addictions can develop distance between craving and behaviour, and chronic pain sufferers can disconnect their pain from its emotional overlay.[7–9]

Mindfulness training also means that in the same way that school children are taught not to believe everything they first hear, they can also learn not to believe everything they first think and feel.[10] Our workplaces too can be transformed by employers, employees and colleagues with better ability to respond rather than react.[11] At a time when there's only one psychiatrist available on average per 100 000 people in over half the countries in the world, mindfulness looks pretty darn promising to me.[12]

In this moment, with all that has preceded in my life and all that is uncertain ahead, I do wonder how different my life would be if I'd been taught this skill at a much younger age ... and what the impact would be for my children's generation on things like family life, education, healthcare and politics if more clear-minded people knew how to notice deeply and respond wisely.

I don't think for one second that mindfulness is a panacea that will solve all the world's problems. But it is a simple skill that helps us to understand how our minds work, and that changes *everything*.

ENDNOTES

Introduction: Now and Zen

1. Blake W. *All Religions Are One*.; 1788.
2. Patel V, Saxena S, Lund C, et al. The Lancet Commission on global mental health and sustainable development. *The Lancet*. 2018;392(10157):1553-1598. doi:10.1016/S0140-6736(18)31612-X
3. World Health Organisation. *Depression: A Global Crisis*.; 2012.
4. World Health Organisation. *Preventing Suicide: A Global Imperative*. World Health Organisation; 2014.
5. Keyes CLM. The mental health continuum: from languishing to flourishing in life. *J Health Soc Behav*. 2002;43(2):207-222.
6. Harvey S. There is NO Secret – How I Learned The Truth About Big Wellness The Hard Way. *The Whole Health Life Blog*. Published July 28, 2017. Accessed May 19, 2020. https://www.shannonharvey.com/blogs/blog/there-is-no-secret-how-i-learned-the-hard-way
7. Mindfulness journal articles published by year: 1980-2019. American Mindfulness Research Association. Published 2020. Accessed May 19, 2020. https://goamra.org/resources/
8. Hilton L, Hempel S, Ewing BA, et al. Mindfulness Meditation for Chronic Pain: Systematic Review and Meta-analysis. *Ann Behav Med*. 2017;51(2):199-213. doi:10.1007/s12160-016-9844-2
9. Khoury B, Sharma M, Rush SE, Fournier C. Mindfulness-based stress reduction for healthy individuals: A meta-analysis. *Journal of Psychosomatic Research*. 2015;78(6):519-528. doi:10.1016/j.jpsychores.2015.03.009

10. Goyal M, Singh S, Sibinga EMS, et al. Meditation programs for psychological stress and well-being: a systematic review and meta-analysis. [Review]. *JAMA Internal Medicine.* 2014;174(3):357-368. doi:10.1001/jamainternmed.2013.13018

11. Sancho M, De Gracia M, Rodríguez RC, et al. Mindfulness-Based Interventions for the Treatment of Substance and Behavioral Addictions: A Systematic Review. *Front Psychiatry.* 2018;9. doi:10.3389/fpsyt.2018.00095

Chapter One: No Time Like the Present

1. Pickert K. The Mindful Revolution. *Time.* Published online February 3, 2014. Accessed May 19, 2020. http://content.time.com/time/magazine/article/0,9171,2163560,00.html

2. Khoury B, Sharma M, Rush SE, Fournier C. Mindfulness-based stress reduction for healthy individuals: A meta-analysis. *Journal of Psychosomatic Research.* 2015;78(6):519-528. doi:10.1016/j.jpsychores.2015.03.009

3. Pickert K., *Op cit.*

4. Hassed C. Mind-Body Medicine: Science, Practice and Philosophy. Published online 2006. http://www.lifestyleandculturelectures.org/lectures/mindfulness/MindBodyMedicine.pdf

5. Pascual-Leone A, Nguyet D, Cohen LG, Brasil-Neto JP, Cammarota A, Hallett M. Modulation of muscle responses evoked by transcranial magnetic stimulation during the acquisition of new fine motor skills. *J Neurophysiol.* 1995;74(3):1037-1045. doi:10.1152/jn.1995.74.3.1037

6. Maguire EA, Gadian DG, Johnsrude IS, et al. Navigation-related structural change in the hippocampi of taxi drivers. *Proceedings of the National Academy of Sciences.* 2000;97(8):4398-4403. doi:10.1073/pnas.070039597

7. Luders E, Cherbuin N, Gaser C. Estimating brain age using high-resolution pattern recognition: Younger brains in long-term meditation practitioners. *Neuroimage.* 2016;134:508-513. doi:10.1016/j.neuroimage.2016.04.007

8. Sternberg RJ. Intelligence. *Dialogues Clin Neurosci.* 2012;14(1):19-27.

9. Walsh R. What is Wisdom? Cross-Cultural and Cross-Disciplinary Syntheses. *Review of General Psychology*. 2015;19(3):278-293. doi:10.1037/gpr0000045

10. Kabat-Zinn J. Too Early to Tell: The Potential Impact and Challenges—Ethical and Otherwise—Inherent in the Mainstreaming of Dharma in an Increasingly Dystopian World. *Mindfulness*. 2017;8(5):1125-1135. doi:10.1007/s12671-017-0758-2

11. Middlebrooks PG, Sommer MA. Neuronal Correlates of Metacognition in Primate Frontal Cortex. *Neuron*. 2012;75(3):517-530. doi:10.1016/j.neuron.2012.05.028

12. Musser G. Time on the Brain: How You Are Always Living In the Past, and Other Quirks of Perception. *Scientific American Blog Network*. Published 2011. Accessed May 19, 2020. https://blogs.scientificamerican.com/observations/time-on-the-brain-how-you-are-always-living-in-the-past-and-other-quirks-of-perception/

13. Villamil A, Vogel T, Weisbaum E, Siegel D. Cultivating Well-Being through the Three Pillars of Mind Training: Understanding How Training the Mind Improves Physiological and Psychological Well-Being. *OBM Integrative and Complementary Medicine*. 2018;4:1-1. doi:10.21926/obm.icm.1901003

14. Harris D. Ten Percent Happier with Dan Harris: Tim Ferriss. *Ten Percent Happier with Dan Harris*. Published February 3, 2018. Accessed May 19, 2020. https://podcastnotes.org/tim-ferris-show/10-happier-with-dan-harris-tim-ferriss/

15. Norcross JC, Mrykalo MS, Blagys MD. Auld Lang Syne: Success predictors, change processes, and self-reported outcomes of New Year's resolvers and nonresolvers. *Journal of Clinical Psychology*. 2002;58(4):397-405. doi:10.1002/jclp.1151

16. Norcross JC, Vangarelli DJ. The resolution solution: longitudinal examination of New Year's change attempts. *J Subst Abuse*. 1988;1(2):127-134. doi:10.1016/s0899-3289(88)80016-6

17. Kwasnicka D, Dombrowski SU, White M, Sniehotta F. Theoretical explanations for maintenance of behaviour change: a systematic

review of behaviour theories. *Health Psychology Review.* 2016;10(3):277-296. doi:10.1080/17437199.2016.1151372

18. Gollwitzer PM, Sheeran P. Implementation Intentions and Goal Achievement: A Meta-analysis of Effects and Processes. In: *Advances in Experimental Social Psychology.* Vol 38. Academic Press; 2006:69-119. doi:10.1016/S0065-2601(06)38002-1

19. Zhang Y, Cooke R. Using a combined motivational and volitional intervention to promote exercise and healthy dietary behaviour among undergraduates. *Diabetes Research and Clinical Practice.* 2012;95(2):215-223. doi:10.1016/j.diabres.2011.10.006

20. Schelling TC. *Strategies of Commitment and Other Essays.* Harvard University Press; 2007.

Chapter Two: Mind the Hype

1. Meditation is the Fastest Growing Health Trend in America. Mindful. Published December 11, 2018. Accessed May 19, 2020. https://www.mindful.org/meditation-is-the-fastest-growing-health-trend-in-america/

2. Marketdata Enterprises. $1.2 Billion U.S. Meditation Market To Grow Strongly, Following Path of Yoga Studios. Published 2017. Accessed May 19, 2020. https://www.marketdataenterprises.com/wp-content/uploads/2018/03/Meditation-Mkt-2017-Press-Release.pdf

3. *KFC | Welcome to the Comfort Zone.* Youtube; 2018. Accessed May 19, 2020. https://www.youtube.com/watch?v=-kpiqOGpho4

4. Turnbull L, Dawson G. Is mindfulness the new opiate of the masses? Critical reflections from a Buddhist perspective. *Psychotherapy in Australia.* 2006;12(4):60.

5. Purser R, Ng E. Corporate mindfulness is bullsh*t: Zen or no Zen, you're working harder and being paid less. *Salon.* Published online 2015. Accessed May 19, 2020. https://www.salon.com/2015/09/27/corporate_mindfulness_is_bullsht_zen_or_no_zen_youre_working_harder_and_being_paid_less/

6. Purser R, Loy D. Beyond McMindfulness. *HuffPost.* Published online 2013. Accessed May 19, 2020. https://www.huffpost.com/entry/beyond-mcmindfulness_b_3519289

7. Purser R. The mindfulness conspiracy. *The Guardian.* https://www.theguardian.com/lifeandstyle/2019/jun/14/the-mindfulness-conspiracy-capitalist-spirituality. Published June 14, 2019. Accessed May 19, 2020.

8. Huxley A. *Complete Essays: 1926-1929.* Ivan R. Dee; 2000.

9. Wright R. Is Mindfulness Meditation BS? *Wired.* Published online August 12, 2017. Accessed May 21, 2020. https://www.wired.com/2017/08/the-science-and-philosophy-of-mindfulness-meditation/

10. Sheridan K. "Mindfulness" is a meaningless word with shoddy science behind it. *Newsweek.* Published October 11, 2017. Accessed May 21, 2020. https://www.newsweek.com/mindfulness-meaningless-word-shoddy-science-behind-it-682008

11. Christopher MS, Charoensuk S, Gilbert BD, Neary TJ, Pearce KL. Mindfulness in Thailand and the United States: a case of apples versus oranges? *Journal of Clinical Psychology.* 2009;65(6):590-612. doi:10.1002/jclp.20580

12. Van Dam NT, van Vugt MK, Vago DR, et al. Mind the Hype: A Critical Evaluation and Prescriptive Agenda for Research on Mindfulness and Meditation. *Perspect Psychol Sci.* 2018;13(1):36-61. doi:10.1177/1745691617709589

13. Firth J, Marx W, Dash S, et al. The Effects of Dietary Improvement on Symptoms of Depression and Anxiety: A Meta-Analysis of Randomized Controlled Trials. *Psychosom Med.* 2019;81(3):265-280. doi:10.1097/PSY.0000000000000673

14. Blanck P, Perleth S, Heidenreich T, et al. Effects of mindfulness exercises as stand-alone intervention on symptoms of anxiety and depression: Systematic review and meta-analysis. *Behaviour Research and Therapy.* 2018;102:25-35. doi:10.1016/j.brat.2017.12.002

15. Lindahl JR, Fisher NE, Cooper DJ, Rosen RK, Britton WB. The varieties of contemplative experience: A mixed-methods study of

meditation-related challenges in Western Buddhists. *PLoS ONE*. 2017;12(5):e0176239. doi:10.1371/journal.pone.0176239

16. Britton WB, Davis JH, Loucks EB, et al. Dismantling Mindfulness-Based Cognitive Therapy: Creation and validation of 8-week focused attention and open monitoring interventions within a 3-armed randomized controlled trial. *Behaviour Research and Therapy*. 2018;101:92-107. doi:10.1016/j.brat.2017.09.010

17. Petticrew MP, Lee K. The "Father of Stress" Meets "Big Tobacco": Hans Selye and the Tobacco Industry. *Am J Public Health*. 2011;101(3):411-418. doi:10.2105/AJPH.2009.177634

Chapter Three: It's *Not* the Thought That Counts

1. Riedel S. Edward Jenner and the history of smallpox and vaccination. *Proc (Bayl Univ Med Cent)*. 2005;18(1):21-25.

2. World Health Organisation. "Depression: let's talk"; says WHO, as depression tops list of causes of ill health. Published 2017. Accessed May 21, 2020. https://www.who.int/news-room/detail/30-03-2017--depression-let-s-talk-says-who-as-depression-tops-list-of-causes-of-ill-health

3. World Health Organisation. Depression. Published 2020. Accessed May 21, 2020. https://www.who.int/news-room/fact-sheets/detail/depression

4. World Health Organisation. Suicide: one person dies every 40 seconds. Published 2019. Accessed May 21, 2020. https://www.who.int/news-room/detail/09-09-2019-suicide-one-person-dies-every-40-seconds

5. University of Oxford. 2019 Most Highly Cited Researchers — University of Oxford, Medical Sciences Division. Published 2019. Accessed May 21, 2020. https://www.medsci.ox.ac.uk/news/2019-most-highly-cited-researchers

6. Burcusa SL, Iacono WG. Risk for Recurrence in Depression. *Clin Psychol Rev*. 2007;27(8):959-985. doi:10.1016/j.cpr.2007.02.005

7. NHS. *The Five Year Forward View for Mental Health: A Report from the Independent Mental Health Taskforce to the NHS in England.*; 2016. https://

www.england.nhs.uk/wp-content/uploads/2016/02/Mental-Health-Taskforce-FYFV-final.pdf

8. MQ: Transforming Mental Health. *UK Mental Health Research Funding.*; 2019. Accessed May 21, 2020. https://s3.eu-central-1.amazonaws.com/ www.joinmq.org/UK+Mental+Health+Research+Funding+2014-2017+digital.pdf

9. Centre for Mental Health. *The Economic and Social Costs of Mental Health Problems.*; 2010. Accessed May 21, 2020. https://www. centreformentalhealth.org.uk/sites/default/files/2018-09/Economic_and_social_costs_2010_0.pdf

10. Kuyken W, Warren FC, Taylor RS, et al. Efficacy of Mindfulness-Based Cognitive Therapy in Prevention of Depressive Relapse: An Individual Patient Data Meta-analysis From Randomized Trials. *JAMA Psychiatry.* 2016;73(6):565-574. doi:10.1001/ jamapsychiatry.2016.0076

11. Hillhouse TM, Porter JH. A brief history of the development of antidepressant drugs: From monoamines to glutamate. *Exp Clin Psychopharmacol.* 2015;23(1):1-21. doi:10.1037/a0038550

12. Hofmann SG, Sawyer AT, Fang A. The Empirical Status of the "New Wave" of CBT. *Psychiatr Clin North Am.* 2010;33(3):701-710. doi:10.1016/j.psc.2010.04.006

13. Birkett MA. The Trier Social Stress Test Protocol for Inducing Psychological Stress. *J Vis Exp.* 2011;(56). doi:10.3791/3238

14. Carney CE, Edinger JD, Meyer B, Lindman L, Istre T. Symptom-focused rumination and sleep disturbance. *Behav Sleep Med.* 2006;4(4):228-241. doi:10.1207/s15402010bsm0404_3

15. Katic B, Heywood J, Turek F, et al. New approach for analyzing self-reporting of insomnia symptoms reveals a high rate of comorbid insomnia across a wide spectrum of chronic diseases. *Sleep Medicine.* 2015;16(11):1332-1341. doi:10.1016/j.sleep.2015.07.024

16. Ohayon MM, Reynolds CF. Epidemiological and clinical relevance of insomnia diagnosis algorithms according to the DSM-IV and the

International Classification of Sleep Disorders (ICSD). *Sleep Med.* 2009;10(9):952-960. doi:10.1016/j.sleep.2009.07.008

17. Colten HR, Altevogt BM. Sleep Disorders and Sleep Deprivation: An Unmet Public Health Problem. *Institute of Medicine (US) Committee on Sleep Medicine and Research. Washington (DC): National Academies Press (US).* 2006;3. https://ncbi.nlm.nih.gov/books/NBK19961. Accessed May 21, 2020.

18. Lundh LG, Broman JE. Insomnia as an interaction between sleep-interfering and sleep-interpreting processes. *J Psychosom Res.* 2000;49(5):299-310. doi:10.1016/s0022-3999(00)00150-1

19. Garland SN, Zhou ES, Gonzalez BD, Rodriguez N. The Quest for Mindful Sleep: A Critical Synthesis of the Impact of Mindfulness-Based Interventions for Insomnia. *Curr Sleep Med Rep.* 2016;2(3):142-151. doi:10.1007/s40675-016-0050-3

20. Gross CR, Kreitzer MJ, Reilly-Spong M, et al. Mindfulness-Based Stress Reduction vs. Pharmacotherapy for Primary Chronic Insomnia: A Pilot Randomized Controlled Clinical Trial. *Explore (NY).* 2011;7(2):76-87. doi:10.1016/j.explore.2010.12.003

21. Kazdin AE. Mediators and mechanisms of change in psychotherapy research. *Annu Rev Clin Psychol.* 2007;3:1-27. doi:10.1146/annurev. clinpsy.3.022806.091432

22. Lutz A, Slagter HA, Dunne JD, Davidson RJ. Attention regulation and monitoring in meditation. *Trends in Cognitive Sciences.* 2008;12(4):163-169. doi:10.1016/j.tics.2008.01.005

23. Brown KW, Ryan RM. The benefits of being present: mindfulness and its role in psychological well-being. *J Pers Soc Psychol.* 2003;84(4):822-848. doi:10.1037/0022-3514.84.4.822

24. Tarrasch R. Mindful Schooling: Better Attention Regulation Among Elementary School Children Who Practice Mindfulness as Part of Their School Policy. *J Cogn Enhanc.* 2017;1(2):84-95. doi:10.1007/s41465-017-0024-5

25. Tang R, Braver TS. Towards an Individual Differences Perspective

in Mindfulness Training Research: Theoretical and Empirical Considerations. *Front Psychol.* 2020;11. doi:10.3389/fpsyg.2020.00818

26. Gross JJ. The Emerging Field of Emotion Regulation: An Integrative Review: *Review of General Psychology.* Published online September 1, 1998. Accessed June 12, 2020. https://journals.sagepub.com/doi/10.1037/1089-2680.2.3.271

27. Gross JJ, John OP. Individual differences in two emotion regulation processes: Implications for affect, relationships, and well-being. *Journal of Personality and Social Psychology.* 20030728;85(2):348. doi:10.1037/0022-3514.85.2.348

28. Guendelman S, Medeiros S, Rampes H. Mindfulness and Emotion Regulation: Insights from Neurobiological, Psychological, and Clinical Studies. *Front Psychol.* 2017;8. doi:10.3389/fpsyg.2017.00220

29. Chambers R, Gullone E, Allen NB. Mindful emotion regulation: An integrative review. *Clinical Psychology Review.* 2009;29(6):560-572. doi:10.1016/j.cpr.2009.06.005

30. Vago DRPD, David SAMD. Self-awareness, self-regulation, and self-transcendence (S-ART): a framework for understanding the neurobiological mechanisms of mindfulness. *Front Hum Neurosci.* 2012;6. doi:10.3389/fnhum.2012.00296

31. Ong JC, Ulmer CS, Manber R. Improving Sleep with Mindfulness and Acceptance: A Metacognitive Model of Insomnia. *Behav Res Ther.* 2012;50(11):651-660. doi:10.1016/j.brat.2012.08.001

32. Shapiro SL, Carlson LE, Astin JA, Freedman B. Mechanisms of mindfulness. *Journal of Clinical Psychology.* 2006;62(3):373-386. doi:10.1002/jclp.20237

33. Safran J, Segal ZV. *Interpersonal Process in Cognitive Therapy.* Jason Aronson, Incorporated; 1996.

34. Fresco DM, Segal ZV, Buis T, Kennedy S. Relationship of posttreatment decentering and cognitive reactivity to relapse in major depression. *Journal of Consulting and Clinical Psychology.* 20070611;75(3):447. doi:10.1037/0022-006X.75.3.447

35. Bernstein A, Hadash Y, Lichtash Y, Tanay G, Shepherd K, Fresco DM. Decentering and Related Constructs: A Critical Review and Metacognitive Processes Model. *Perspect Psychol Sci*. 2015;10(5):599-617. doi:10.1177/1745691615594577

36. Teasdale JD, Moore RG, Hayhurst H, Pope M, Williams S, Segal ZV. Metacognitive awareness and prevention of relapse in depression: empirical evidence. *J Consult Clin Psychol*. 2002;70(2):275-287. doi:10.1037//0022-006x.70.2.275

37. van der Velden AM, Kuyken W, Wattar U, et al. A systematic review of mechanisms of change in mindfulness-based cognitive therapy in the treatment of recurrent major depressive disorder. *Clinical Psychology Review*. 2015;37:26-39. doi:10.1016/j.cpr.2015.02.001

38. Lindsay EK, Creswell JD. Mechanisms of mindfulness training: Monitor and Acceptance Theory (MAT). *Clin Psychol Rev*. 2017;51:48–59. doi:10.1016/j.cpr.2016.10.011

39. Ford BQ, Lam P, John OP, Mauss IB. The psychological health benefits of accepting negative emotions and thoughts: Laboratory, diary, and longitudinal evidence. *Journal of Personality and Social Psychology*. 20170713;115(6):1075. doi:10.1037/pspp0000157

40. (Bud) Craig AD. How do you feel — now? The anterior insula and human awareness. *Nature Reviews Neuroscience*. 2009;10(1):59-70. doi:10.1038/nrn2555

41. Khoury B, Knäuper B, Pagnini F, Trent N, Chiesa A, Carrière K. Embodied Mindfulness. *Mindfulness*. 2017;8(5):1160-1171. doi:10.1007/s12671-017-0700-7

42. Gibson J. Mindfulness, Interoception, and the Body: A Contemporary Perspective. *Front Psychol*. 2019;10. doi:10.3389/fpsyg.2019.02012

43. Eggart M, Lange A, Binser MJ, Queri S, Müller-Oerlinghausen B. Major Depressive Disorder Is Associated with Impaired Interoceptive Accuracy: A Systematic Review. *Brain Sci*. 2019;9(6):131. Published 2019 Jun 6. doi:10.3390/brainsci9060131

44. Vago DRPD, David SAMD. *Op cit*.

45. Yeats WB. *Mosada: 'If Suffering Brings Wisdom, I Would Wish to Be Less Wise.'* Stage Door; 2013.

46. Brewer JA, Mallik S, Babuscio TA, et al. Mindfulness training for smoking cessation: results from a randomized controlled trial. *Drug Alcohol Depend.* 2011;119(1-2):72-80. doi:10.1016/j.drugalcdep.2011.05.027

47. Blakeslee S. Nicotine: Harder to Kick...than Heroin. *The New York Times.* https://www.nytimes.com/1987/03/29/magazine/nicotine-harder-to-kickthan-heroin.html. Published March 29, 1987. Accessed May 21, 2020.

48. United Nations Office on Drugs and Crime. *World Drug Report 2018.*; 2018.

49. National Institute on Drug Abuse. Drug Use: Trends & Statistics. Published February 6, 2020. Accessed May 21, 2020. https://www.drugabuse.gov/related-topics/trends-statistics

50. Maisto SA, Pollock NK, Cornelius JR, Lynch KG, Martin CS. Alcohol relapse as a function of relapse definition in a clinical sample of adolescents. *Addict Behav.* 2003;28(3):449-459. doi:10.1016/s0306-4603(01)00267-2

51. Witkiewitz K, Masyn KE. Drinking trajectories following an initial lapse. *Psychol Addict Behav.* 2008;22(2):157-167. doi:10.1037/0893-164X.22.2.157

52. Li W, Howard MO, Garland EL, McGovern P, Lazar M. Mindfulness treatment for substance misuse: A systematic review and meta-analysis. *Journal of Substance Abuse Treatment.* 2017;75:62-96. doi:10.1016/j.jsat.2017.01.008

53. Chiesa A, Serretti A. Are mindfulness-based interventions effective for substance use disorders? A systematic review of the evidence. *Subst Use Misuse.* 2014;49(5):492-512. doi:10.3109/10826084.2013.770027

Chapter Four: Mindful Medicine

1. Do Not Be So Open-Minded That Your Brains Fall Out – Quote Investigator. Accessed June 8, 2020. https://quoteinvestigator.com/2014/04/13/open-mind/

2. Khaddouma A, Coop Gordon K, Strand EB. Mindful Mates: A Pilot Study of the Relational Effects of Mindfulness-Based Stress Reduction on Participants and Their Partners. *Fam Process*. 2017;56(3):636-651. doi:10.1111/famp.12226

3. Hoge EA, Bui E, Palitz SA, et al. The effect of mindfulness meditation training on biological acute stress responses in generalized anxiety disorder. *Psychiatry Res*. 2018;262:328-332. doi:10.1016/j.psychres.2017.01.006

4. Hoge EA, Bui E, Marques L, et al. Randomized Controlled Trial of Mindfulness Meditation for Generalized Anxiety Disorder: Effects on Anxiety and Stress Reactivity. *J Clin Psychiatry*. 2013;74(8):786-792. doi:10.4088/JCP.12m08083

5. Vignaud P, Donde C, Sadki T, Poulet E, Brunelin J. Neural effects of mindfulness-based interventions on patients with major depressive disorder: A systematic review. *Neurosci Biobehav Rev*. 2018;88:98-105. doi:10.1016/j.neubiorev.2018.03.004

6. Reiner K, Tibi L, Lipsitz JD. Do mindfulness-based interventions reduce pain intensity? A critical review of the literature. *Pain Medicine*. 2013;14(2):230-242. doi:10.1111/pme.12006

7. Sanada K, Alda Díez M, Salas Valero M, et al. Effects of mindfulness-based interventions on biomarkers in healthy and cancer populations: a systematic review. *BMC Complement Altern Med*. 2017;17(1):125. doi:10.1186/s12906-017-1638-y

8. Sevinc G, Hölzel BK, Hashmi J, et al. Common and Dissociable Neural Activity After Mindfulness-Based Stress Reduction and Relaxation Response Programs. *Psychosom Med*. 2018;80(5):439-451. doi:10.1097/PSY.0000000000000590

9. Hölzel BK, Carmody J, Vangel M, et al. Mindfulness practice leads to increases in regional brain gray matter density. *Psychiatry Res*. 2011;191(1):36-43. doi:10.1016/j.pscychresns.2010.08.006

10. Mindfulness meditation and relaxation response affect brain differently. *Harvard Gazette*. Published June 20, 2018. Accessed May 23,

2020. https://news.harvard.edu/gazette/story/2018/06/mindfulness-meditation-and-relaxation-response-affect-brain-differently/

11. Britton WB, Davis JH, Loucks EB, et al. Dismantling Mindfulness-Based Cognitive Therapy: Creation and validation of 8-week focused attention and open monitoring interventions within a 3-armed randomized controlled trial. *Behaviour Research and Therapy*. 2018;101:92-107. doi:10.1016/j.brat.2017.09.010

12. MacCoon DG, Imel ZE, Rosenkranz MA, et al. The validation of an active control intervention for Mindfulness Based Stress Reduction (MBSR). *Behaviour Research and Therapy*. 2012;50(1):3-12. doi:10.1016/j.brat.2011.10.011

13. *Ibid.*

14. Goldberg SB, Wielgosz J, Dahl C, et al. Does the Five Facet Mindfulness Questionnaire measure what we think it does? Construct validity evidence from an active controlled randomized clinical trial. *Psychol Assess*. 2016;28(8):1009-1014. doi:10.1037/pas0000233

15. Grepmair L, Mitterlehner F, Loew T, Bachler E, Rother W, Nickel M. Promoting mindfulness in psychotherapists in training influences the treatment results of their patients: a randomized, double-blind, controlled study. *Psychother Psychosom*. 2007;76(6):332-338. doi:10.1159/000107560

16. Kurdyak P, Newman A, Segal Z. Impact of mindfulness-based cognitive therapy on health care utilization: a population-based controlled comparison. *J Psychosom Res*. 2014;77(2):85-89. doi:10.1016/j.jpsychores.2014.06.009

17. MacCoon DG, Imel ZE, Rosenkranz MA, et al. *Op cit.*

18. Rosenkranz MA, Davidson RJ, MacCoon DG, Sheridan JF, Kalin NH, Lutz A. A comparison of mindfulness-based stress reduction and an active control in modulation of neurogenic inflammation. *Brain, Behavior, and Immunity*. 2013;27

19. Hilton L, Hempel S, Ewing BA, et al. Mindfulness Meditation for Chronic Pain: Systematic Review and Meta-analysis. *Ann Behav Med*. 2017;51(2):199-213. doi:10.1007/s12160-016-9844-2

20. Grossman P, Tiefenthaler-Gilmer U, Raysz A, Kesper U. Mindfulness training as an intervention for fibromyalgia: evidence of postintervention and 3-year follow-up benefits in well-being. *Psychotherapy & Psychosomatics*. 2007;76(4):226-233. doi:10.1159/000101501

21. Cherkin DC, Sherman KJ, Balderson BH, et al. Effect of Mindfulness-Based Stress Reduction vs Cognitive Behavioral Therapy or Usual Care on Back Pain and Functional Limitations in Adults With Chronic Low Back Pain: A Randomized Clinical Trial. *JAMA*. 2016;315(12):1240-1249. doi:10.1001/jama.2016.2323

22. Wells RE, Burch R, Paulsen RH, Wayne PM, Houle TT, Loder E. Meditation for migraines: a pilot randomized controlled trial. *Headache*. 2014;54(9):1484-1495. doi:10.1111/head.12420

23. Fox SD, Flynn E, Allen RH. Mindfulness meditation for women with chronic pelvic pain: a pilot study. *Journal of Reproductive Medicine*. 2011;56(3-4):158-162.

Chapter Five: Discomfortable

1. Nelson P. *There's a Hole in My Sidewalk: The Romance of Self-Discovery*. 2 edition. Atria Books/Beyond Words; 1994.

2. ASAM Definition of Addiction. Accessed June 8, 2020. https://www.asam.org/Quality-Science/definition-of-addiction

3. National Academies of Sciences E, Division H and M, Policy B on HS, et al. *Pain Management and the Intersection of Pain and Opioid Use Disorder*. National Academies Press (US); 2017. Accessed May 23, 2020. https://www.ncbi.nlm.nih.gov/books/NBK458655/

4. Nahin RL. Estimates of Pain Prevalence and Severity in Adults: United States, 2012. *J Pain*. 2015;16(8):769-780. doi:10.1016/j.jpain.2015.05.002

5. Gaskin DJ, Richard P. *The Economic Costs of Pain in the United States*. National Academies Press (US); 2011. Accessed May 23, 2020. https://www.ncbi.nlm.nih.gov/books/NBK92521/

6. Fayaz A, Croft P, Langford RM, Donaldson LJ, Jones GT. Prevalence of chronic pain in the UK: a systematic review and meta-analysis

of population studies. *BMJ Open*. 2016;6(6):e010364. doi:10.1136/bmjopen-2015-010364

7. Henderson JV, Harrison CM, Britt HC, Bayram CF, Miller GC. Prevalence, Causes, Severity, Impact, and Management of Chronic Pain in Australian General Practice Patients. *Pain Med*. 2013;14(9):1346-1361. doi:10.1111/pme.12195

8. Dueñas M, Ojeda B, Salazar A, Mico JA, Failde I. A review of chronic pain impact on patients, their social environment and the health care system. *J Pain Res*. 2016;9:457-467. doi:10.2147/JPR.S105892

9. Sheng J, Liu S, Wang Y, Cui R, Zhang X. The Link between Depression and Chronic Pain: Neural Mechanisms in the Brain. *Neural Plast*. 2017;2017. doi:10.1155/2017/9724371

10. Bair MJ, Robinson RL, Katon W, Kroenke K. Depression and pain comorbidity: a literature review. *Arch Intern Med*. 2003;163(20):2433-2445. doi:10.1001/archinte.163.20.2433

11. Williams LS, Jones WJ, Shen J, Robinson RL, Weinberger M, Kroenke K. Prevalence and impact of depression and pain in neurology outpatients. *J Neurol Neurosurg Psychiatry*. 2003;74(11):1587-1589. doi:10.1136/jnnp.74.11.1587

12. Sallatha Sutta: The Arrow. Accessed June 8, 2020. https://www.accesstoinsight.org/tipitaka/sn/sn36/sn36.006.than.html

13. Peddareddygari LR, Oberoi K, Grewal RP. Congenital Insensitivity to Pain: A Case Report and Review of the Literature. *Case Rep Neurol Med*. 2014;2014. doi:10.1155/2014/141953

14. Schon K, Parker A, Woods CG. Congenital Insensitivity to Pain Overview. In: Adam MP, Ardinger HH, Pagon RA, et al., eds. *GeneReviews®*. University of Washington, Seattle; 1993. Accessed May 23, 2020. http://www.ncbi.nlm.nih.gov/books/NBK481553/

15. Cohen Marill M. The Unseen Victims of the Opioid Crisis Are Starting to Rebel. *Wired*. Published online 2019. Accessed May 23, 2020. https://www.wired.com/story/the-true-victims-of-the-opioid-crisis-are-starting-to-rebel/

16. Ho KY, Gwee KA, Cheng YK, Yoon KH, Hee HT, Omar AR. Nonsteroidal anti-inflammatory drugs in chronic pain: implications of new data for clinical practice. *J Pain Res.* 2018;11:1937-1948. doi:10.2147/JPR.S168188

17. U.S. Department of Health & Human Services. Facing Addiction in America: The Surgeon General's Report on Alcohol, Drugs, and Health. Published online 2016:413.

18. Alexander GC, Kruszewski SP, Webster DW. Rethinking Opioid Prescribing to Protect Patient Safety and Public Health. *JAMA.* 2012;308(18):1865-1866. doi:10.1001/jama.2012.14282

19. NIMHD. Opioid Epidemic. NIMHD. Published 2020. Accessed May 23, 2020. https://www.nimhd.nih.gov/programs/extramural/ investigator-initiated-research/opioid-epidemic.html

20. Breivik H, Collett B, Ventafridda V, Cohen R, Gallacher D. Survey of chronic pain in Europe: prevalence, impact on daily life, and treatment. *Eur J Pain.* 2006;10(4):287-333. doi:10.1016/j. ejpain.2005.06.009

21. Yokell MA, Delgado MK, Zaller ND, Wang NE, McGowan SK, Green TC. Presentation of Prescription and Nonprescription Opioid Overdoses to US Emergency Departments. *JAMA Intern Med.* 2014;174(12):2034-2037. doi:10.1001/jamainternmed.2014.5413

22. Taylor S, Annand F, Burkinshaw P, et al. Dependence and withdrawal associated with some prescribed medicines: an evidence review. *Public Health England.* Published online 2019:152.

23. Dueñas M, Ojeda B, Salazar A, Mico JA, Failde I. *Op cit.*

24. Treede R-D, Rief W, Barke A, et al. Chronic pain as a symptom or a disease: the IASP Classification of Chronic Pain for the International Classification of Diseases (ICD-11). *PAIN.* 2019;160(1):19–27. doi:10.1097/j.pain.0000000000001384

25. Raffaeli W, Arnaudo E. Pain as a disease: an overview. *J Pain Res.* 2017;10:2003-2008. doi:10.2147/JPR.S138864

26. Davis N. Chronic pain: prescribe mental health support as well as drugs, say experts. *The Guardian.* Published February 5, 2020.

Accessed May 23, 2020. https://www.theguardian.com/society/2020/
feb/05/chronic-pain-prescribe-mental-health-support-as-well-as-
drugs-say-experts.

27. Chiesa A, Serretti A. Mindfulness-based interventions for chronic
pain: a systematic review of the evidence. [Review]. *Journal of
Alternative and Complementary Medicine*. 2011;17(1):83-93. doi:10.1089/
acm.2009.0546

28. Kabat-Zinn J. An outpatient program in behavioral medicine for
chronic pain patients based on the practice of mindfulness meditation:
theoretical considerations and preliminary results. *General Hospital
Psychiatry*. 1982;4(1):33-47.

29. Kabat-Zinn J, Lipworth L, Burney R. The clinical use of mindfulness
meditation for the self-regulation of chronic pain. *Journal of Behavioral
Medicine*. 1985;8(2):163-190.

30. Hilton L, Hempel S, Ewing BA, et al. Mindfulness Meditation for
Chronic Pain: Systematic Review and Meta-analysis. *Ann Behav Med*.
2017;51(2):199-213. doi:10.1007/s12160-016-9844-2

31. Jacob JA. As Opioid Prescribing Guidelines Tighten, Mindfulness
Meditation Holds Promise for Pain Relief. *JAMA*. 2016;315(22):2385-
2387. doi:10.1001/jama.2016.4875

32. Gard T, Holzel BK, Sack AT, et al. Pain attenuation through
mindfulness is associated with decreased cognitive control
and increased sensory processing in the brain. *Cerebral Cortex*.
2012;22(11):2692-2702. doi:10.1093/cercor/bhr352

33. Grant JA, Courtemanche J, Rainville P. A non-elaborative mental
stance and decoupling of executive and pain-related cortices predicts
low pain sensitivity in Zen meditators. *Pain*. 2011;152(1):150-156.
doi:10.1016/j.pain.2010.10.006

Chapter Six: Waking Up

1. Xie L, Kang H, Xu Q, et al. Sleep Drives Metabolite Clearance
from the Adult Brain. *Science*. 2013;342(6156). doi:10.1126/
science.1241224

2. Jessen NA, Munk ASF, Lundgaard I, Nedergaard M. The Glymphatic System: A Beginner's Guide. *Neurochem Res*. 2015;40(12):2583-2599. doi:10.1007/s11064-015-1581-6

3. Lazar SW, Kerr CE, Wasserman RH, et al. Meditation experience is associated with increased cortical thickness. *Neuroreport*. 2005;16(17):1893-1897.

4. Hölzel BK, Carmody J, Vangel M, et al. Mindfulness practice leads to increases in regional brain gray matter density. *Psychiatry Res*. 2011;191(1):36-43. doi:10.1016/j.pscychresns.2010.08.006

5. Zeidan F, Johnson SK, Diamond BJ, David Z, Goolkasian P. Mindfulness meditation improves cognition: Evidence of brief mental training. *Consciousness and Cognition*. 2010;19(2):597-605. doi:10.1016/j.concog.2010.03.014

6. Zeidan F, Gordon NS, Merchant J, Goolkasian P. The effects of brief mindfulness meditation training on experimentally induced pain. *Journal of Pain*. 2010;11(3):199-209. doi:10.1016/j.jpain.2009.07.015

7. Andrews S, Ellis D, Shaw H, Piwek L. Beyond Self-Report: Tools to Compare Estimated and Real-World Smartphone Use. *PloS one*. 2015;10:e0139004. doi:10.1371/journal.pone.0139004

8. Duke É, Montag C. Smartphone addiction, daily interruptions and self-reported productivity. *Addict Behav Rep*. 2017;6:90-95. doi:10.1016/j.abrep.2017.07.002

9. Ward AF, Duke K, Gneezy A, Bos MW. Brain Drain: The Mere Presence of One's Own Smartphone Reduces Available Cognitive Capacity. *Journal of the Association for Consumer Research*. 2017;2(2):140-154. doi:10.1086/691462

10. Augner C, Hacker GW. Associations between problematic mobile phone use and psychological parameters in young adults. *Int J Public Health*. 2012;57(2):437-441. doi:10.1007/s00038-011-0234-z

11. Yun H, Kettinger W, Lee C. A New Open Door: The Smartphone's Impact on Work-to-Life Conflict, Stress, and Resistance. *International Journal of Electronic Commerce*. 2012;16:121-152. doi:10.2753/JEC1086-4415160405

12. Exelmans L, Van den Bulck J. Bedtime mobile phone use and sleep in adults. *Soc Sci Med.* 2016;148:93-101. doi:10.1016/j.socscimed.2015.11.037

13. Reid DJ, Reid FJM. Text or talk? Social anxiety, loneliness, and divergent preferences for cell phone use. *Cyberpsychol Behav.* 2007;10(3):424-435. doi:10.1089/cpb.2006.9936

14. Gliklich E, Guo R, Bergmark RW. Texting while driving: A study of 1211 U.S. adults with the Distracted Driving Survey. *Prev Med Rep.* 2016;4:486-489. doi:10.1016/j.pmedr.2016.09.003

15. Staddon JER, Cerutti DT. Operant Conditioning. *Annu Rev Psychol.* 2003;54:115-144. doi:10.1146/annurev.psych.54.101601.145124

16. ASAM Definition of Addiction. Accessed June 8, 2020. https://www.asam.org/Quality-Science/definition-of-addiction

17. *Ibid.*

18. Solon O. Ex-Facebook president Sean Parker: site made to exploit human "vulnerability." *The Guardian.* https://www.theguardian.com/technology/2017/nov/09/facebook-sean-parker-vulnerability-brain-psychology. Published November 9, 2017. Accessed June 8, 2020.

19. Lewis P. "Our minds can be hijacked": the tech insiders who fear a smartphone dystopia. *The Guardian.* https://www.theguardian.com/technology/2017/oct/05/smartphone-addiction-silicon-valley-dystopia. Published October 6, 2017. Accessed May 23, 2020.

20. Edwards J. 'The Evolution of Ev: The creator of Twitter, Blogger, and Medium has a plan to fix the mess he made of the internet' Business Insider. Accessed May 23, 2020. https://www.businessinsider.com.au/evolution-of-ev-williams-and-medium-2018-11?r=US&IR=T

21. The Designer of the iPhone Worries That His Grandkids Will Think He's the Guy 'That Destroyed Society.' Accessed June 8, 2020. https://thriveglobal.com/stories/tony-fadell-iphone-society/

22. Bilton N. Steve Jobs Was a Low-Tech Parent. *The New York Times.* https://www.nytimes.com/2014/09/11/fashion/steve-jobs-apple-was-a-low-tech-parent.html. Published September 10, 2014. Accessed June 8, 2020.

23. De-Sola Gutiérrez J, Rodríguez de Fonseca F, Rubio G. Cell-Phone Addiction: A Review. *Front Psychiatry*. 2016;7. doi:10.3389/fpsyt.2016.00175

24. Kardaras DN. It's 'digital heroin': How screens turn kids into psychotic junkies. *New York Post*. Published August 27, 2016. Accessed May 23, 2020. https://nypost.com/2016/08/27/its-digital-heroin-how-screens-turn-kids-into-psychotic-junkies/

25. Gonzalez R. It's Time For a Serious Talk About the Science of Tech "Addiction." *Wired*. Published online 2018. Accessed May 23, 2020. https://www.wired.com/story/its-time-for-a-serious-talk-about-the-science-of-tech-addiction/

26. Furedi F. Age of Distraction: Why the idea digital devices are destroying our concentration and memory is a myth. *The Independent*. https://www.independent.co.uk/life-style/gadgets-and-tech/features/age-of-distraction-why-the-idea-digital-devices-are-destroying-our-concentration-and-memory-is-a-a6689776.html. Published 2015. Accessed May 23, 2020.

27. Anderson J, Rainie L. The Future of Well-Being in a Tech-Saturated World. *Pew Research Center*; Published 2018. Accessed May 18, 2020. www.pewresearch.org/internet/2018/04/17/the-future-of-well-being-in-a-tech-saturated-world/

28. Lewis P. *Op cit.*

29. Griffiths M. Adolescent mobile phone addiction: A cause for concern? *Education and Health*. 2013;31:76-78.

30. Oliver M. *New And Selected Poems, Volume One: 1*. Reprint edition. Beacon Press; 2018.

31. Montag C, Kannen C, Lachmann B, et al. The importance of analogue zeitgebers to reduce digital addictive tendencies in the 21st century. *Addict Behav Rep*. 2015;2:23-27. doi:10.1016/j.abrep.2015.04.002

32. American Psychological Association. *Stress in America: Coping with Change.*; 2017. Accessed May 23, 2020. https://www.apa.org/news/press/releases/stress/2016/coping-with-change.pdf

Chapter Seven: Not-Self Help

1. Lutz A, Greischar LL, Rawlings NB, Ricard M, Davidson RJ. Long-term meditators self-induce high-amplitude gamma synchrony during mental practice. *Proc Natl Acad Sci U S A.* 2004;101(46):16369-16373. doi:10.1073/pnas.0407401101

2. Amiel HF. *Amiel's Journal: The Journal Intimé of Henri Frédéric Amiel, Tr., with an Introduction and Notes.* A. L. Burt; 1910.

3. Hunter ECM, Charlton J, David AS. Depersonalisation and derealisation: assessment and management. *BMJ.* 2017;356. doi:10.1136/bmj.j745

4. Lofthouse G. Enlightenment's Evil Twin. *The Atlantic.* Published December 16, 2014. Accessed May 23, 2020. https://www.theatlantic.com/health/archive/2014/12/enlightenments-evil-twin/383726/

5. Gunaratana BH. What Exactly is Vipassana Meditation? *Tricycle: The Buddhist Review.* Published 2019. Accessed May 23, 2020. https://tricycle.org/magazine/vipassana-meditation/

6. Access to Insight. A Sketch of the Buddha's Life: Readings from the Pali Canon. Access to Insight. Published 2005. Accessed May 23, 2020. https://www.accesstoinsight.org/ptf/buddha.html

7. Davis J. Who Was Sayadaw U Pandita? *Lion's Roar.* Published October 16, 2018. Accessed May 23, 2020. https://www.lionsroar.com/who-was-sayadaw-u-pandita/

8. Braun E. Meditation en Masse. *Tricycle: The Buddhist Review.* Published 2014. Accessed May 23, 2020. https://tricycle.org/magazine/meditation-en-masse/

9. Gunaratana BH. *Op cit.*

10. *Robert Wright & Joseph Goldstein [The Wright Show] (Full Conversation).*; 2016. Accessed May 23, 2020. https://www.youtube.com/watch?v=p9GgDJw192I&feature=youtu.be

11. Wright R. Making sense of the Buddhist idea that the self doesn't exist. Nonzero.org. Published 2020. Accessed May 23, 2020. https://nonzero.org/post/self-joseph-goldstein

Chapter Eight: From Me to We

1. The Leonard Lopate Show. Behold the Most Complicated Object in the Known Universe. Accessed June 8, 2020. https://www.wnyc.org/story/michio-kaku-explores-human-brain/

2. Burkeman O. Why can't the world's greatest minds solve the mystery of consciousness? | Oliver Burkeman. *The Guardian*. https://www.theguardian.com/science/2015/jan/21/-sp-why-cant-worlds-greatest-minds-solve-mystery-consciousness. Published January 21, 2015. Accessed May 23, 2020.

3. Cobb M. Why your brain is not a computer. *The Guardian*. https://www.theguardian.com/science/2020/feb/27/why-your-brain-is-not-a-computer-neuroscience-neural-networks-consciousness. Published February 27, 2020. Accessed May 23, 2020.

4. Kaku M. The Golden Age of Neuroscience Has Arrived. *Wall Street Journal*. https://www.wsj.com/articles/michio-kaku-the-golden-age-of-neuroscience-has-arrived-1408577023. Published August 20, 2014. Accessed May 23, 2020.

5. Institute of Medicine (US) Committee on a National Neural Circuitry. *Mapping the Brain and Its Functions: Integrating Enabling Technologies into Neuroscience Research*. National Academies Press (US); 1991. Accessed May 23, 2020. https://www.ncbi.nlm.nih.gov/books/NBK234380/

6. Deacon TW. Rethinking Mammalian Brain Evolution. *Integr Comp Biol*. 1990;30(3):629-705. doi:10.1093/icb/30.3.629

7. Nielsen JA, Zielinski BA, Ferguson MA, Lainhart JE, Anderson JS. An Evaluation of the Left-Brain vs. Right-Brain Hypothesis with Resting State Functional Connectivity Magnetic Resonance Imaging. *PLOS ONE*. 2013;8(8):e71275. doi:10.1371/journal.pone.0071275

8. Bressler SL, Menon V. Large-scale brain networks in cognition: emerging methods and principles. *Trends in Cognitive Sciences*. 2010;14(6):277-290. doi:10.1016/j.tics.2010.04.004

9. King AP, Fresco DM. A neurobehavioral account for decentering as the salve for the distressed mind. *Curr Opin Psychol*. 2019;28:285-293. doi:10.1016/j.copsyc.2019.02.009

10. Raichle ME, MacLeod AM, Snyder AZ, Powers WJ, Gusnard DA, Shulman GL. A default mode of brain function. *Proc Natl Acad Sci U S A*. 2001;98(2):676-682.

11. Immordino-Yang MH, Christodoulou JA, Singh V. Rest Is Not Idleness: Implications of the Brain's Default Mode for Human Development and Education. *Perspect Psychol Sci*. 2012;7(4):352-364. doi:10.1177/1745691612447308

12. Andrews-Hanna JR, Reidler JS, Sepulcre J, Poulin R, Buckner RL. Functional-Anatomic Fractionation of the Brain's Default Network. *Neuron*. 2010;65(4):550-562. doi:10.1016/j.neuron.2010.02.005

13. Farb NAS, Segal ZV, Mayberg H, et al. Attending to the present: mindfulness meditation reveals distinct neural modes of self-reference. *Soc Cogn Affect Neurosci*. 2007;2(4):313-322. doi:10.1093/scan/nsm030

14. Gao W, Zhu H, Giovanello KS, et al. Evidence on the emergence of the brain's default network from 2-week-old to 2-year-old healthy pediatric subjects. *Proc Natl Acad Sci USA*. 2009;106(16):6790-6795. doi:10.1073/pnas.0811221106

15. Goetz JL, Keltner D, Simon-Thomas E. Compassion: an evolutionary analysis and empirical review. *Psychol Bull*. 2010;136(3):351-374. doi:10.1037/a0018807

16. Immordino-Yang MH, Christodoulou JA, Singh V. *Op cit*.

17. Killingsworth MA, Gilbert DT. A wandering mind is an unhappy mind. *Science*. 2010;330(6006):932. doi:10.1126/science.1192439

18. Sood A, Jones DT. On Mind Wandering, Attention, Brain Networks, and Meditation. *EXPLORE*. 2013;9(3):136-141. doi:10.1016/j.explore.2013.02.005

19. Ramírez-Barrantes R, Arancibia M, Stojanova J, Aspé-Sánchez M, Córdova C, Henríquez-Ch RA. Default Mode Network, Meditation, and Age-Associated Brain Changes: What Can We Learn from the Impact of Mental Training on Well-Being as a Psychotherapeutic Approach? *Neural Plasticity*. 2019;2019:1-15. doi:10.1155/2019/7067592

20. Broyd SJ, Demanuele C, Debener S, Helps SK, James CJ, Sonuga-Barke EJS. Default-mode brain dysfunction in mental disorders:

a systematic review. *Neurosci Biobehav Rev.* 2009;33(3):279-296. doi:10.1016/j.neubiorev.2008.09.002

21. Hamilton JP, Furman DJ, Chang C, Thomason ME, Dennis E, Gotlib IH. Default-mode and task-positive network activity in major depressive disorder: implications for adaptive and maladaptive rumination. *Biol Psychiatry.* 2011;70(4):327-333. doi:10.1016/j. biopsych.2011.02.003

22. Lombardo MV, Chakrabarti B, Bullmore ET, et al. Atypical neural self-representation in autism. *Brain.* 2010;133(Pt 2):611-624. doi:10.1093/brain/awp306

23. Brewer JA, Worhunsky PD, Gray JR, Tang Y-Y, Weber J, Kober H. Meditation experience is associated with differences in default mode network activity and connectivity. *Proc Natl Acad Sci U S A.* 2011;108(50):20254-20259. doi:10.1073/pnas.1112029108

24. Berkovich-Ohana A, Harel M, Hahamy A, Arieli A, Malach R. Alterations in task-induced activity and resting-state fluctuations in visual and DMN areas revealed in long-term meditators. *Neuroimage.* 2016;135:125-134. doi:10.1016/j.neuroimage.2016.04.024

25. Cotier FA, Zhang R, Lee TMC. A longitudinal study of the effect of short-term meditation training on functional network organization of the aging brain. *Sci Rep.* 2017;7. doi:10.1038/s41598-017-00678-8

26. Taylor VA, Daneault V, Grant J, et al. Impact of meditation training on the default mode network during a restful state. *Soc Cogn Affect Neurosci.* 2013;8(1):4-14. doi:10.1093/scan/nsr087

27. Shao R, Keuper K, Geng X, Lee TMC. Pons to Posterior Cingulate Functional Projections Predict Affective Processing Changes in the Elderly Following Eight Weeks of Meditation Training. *EBioMedicine.* 2016;10:236-248. doi:10.1016/j.ebiom.2016.06.018

28. Brewer JA, Worhunsky PD, Gray JR, Tang Y-Y, Weber J, Kober H. *Op cit.*

29. Garrison KA, Zeffiro TA, Scheinost D, Constable RT, Brewer JA. Meditation leads to reduced default mode network activity beyond an active task. *Cogn Affect Behav Neurosci.* 2015;15(3):712-720. doi:10.3758/s13415-015-0358-3

30. Garrison KA, Santoyo JF, Davis JH, Thornhill TA, Kerr CE, Brewer JA. Effortless awareness: using real time neurofeedback to investigate correlates of posterior cingulate cortex activity in meditators' self-report. *Front Hum Neurosci.* 2013;7. doi:10.3389/fnhum.2013.00440

31. Girardeau G, Benchenane K, Wiener SI, Buzsáki G, Zugaro MB. Selective suppression of hippocampal ripples impairs spatial memory. *Nature Neuroscience.* 2009;12(10):1222-1223. doi:10.1038/nn.2384

32. Baird B, Smallwood J, Mrazek MD, Kam JWY, Franklin MS, Schooler JW. Inspired by Distraction: Mind Wandering Facilitates Creative Incubation. *Psychol Sci.* 2012;23(10):1117-1122. doi:10.1177/0956797612446024

33. Dijksterhuis A, Bos MW, Nordgren LF, Baaren RB van. On Making the Right Choice: The Deliberation-Without-Attention Effect. *Science.* 2006;311(5763):1005-1007. doi:10.1126/science.1121629

34. Barks C. *The Essential Rumi Revised.* Reprint edition. HarperCollins - US; 1997.

35. Einstein A. Condolence letter to Robert S. Marcus. Written February 12, 1950. Accessed online June 8, 2020. https://lettersofnote.com/2011/11/10/the-delusion/

36. *Schrödinger's Cat: A Thought Experiment in Quantum Mechanics - Chad Orzel.*; 2014. Accessed May 23, 2020. https://www.youtube.com/watch?v=UjaAxUO6-Uw

37. Diebels K, Leary M. The Psychological Implications of Believing that Everything is One. *The Journal of Positive Psychology.* Published online June 14, 2018:1-11. doi:10.1080/17439760.2018.1484939

38. Edinger-Schons LM. Oneness beliefs and their effect on life satisfaction. *Psychology of Religion and Spirituality.* Published online April 11, 2019. doi:10.1037/rel0000259

Chapter Nine: Moments of Refuge

1. Shelton T. If Daraa falls, could it be the beginning of the end of the Syrian war? Published June 23, 2018. Accessed May 23, 2020. https://

www.abc.net.au/news/2018-06-23/cradle-of-the-revolution-why-daraa-is-next/9809420

2. Human Rights Watch. World Report 2019: Rights Trends in Syria. Human Rights Watch. Published December 17, 2018. Accessed May 23, 2020. https://www.hrw.org/world-report/2019/country-chapters/syria

3. Silove D, Ventevogel P, Rees S. The contemporary refugee crisis: an overview of mental health challenges. *World Psychiatry.* 2017;16(2):130-139. doi:10.1002/wps.20438

4. The New Arab. Syrian regime jets pound Daraa after rebel attacks. alaraby. Published June 5, 2017. Accessed May 23, 2020. https://english.alaraby.co.uk/english/news/2017/6/5/syrian-regime-jets-pound-a-day-after-rebel-attacks

5. Silove D, Ventevogel P, Rees S. *Op cit.*

6. Reisen MEH van, Rijken CRJJ, Estefanos M. *The Human Trafficking Cycle: Sinai and Beyond.* Wolf Legal Publishers (WLP); 2014. Accessed May 23, 2020. https://research.tilburguniversity.edu/en/publications/the-human-trafficking-cycle-sinai-and-beyond

7. Human Rights Watch. World Report 2018: Rights Trends in Eritrea. Human Rights Watch. Published December 21, 2017. Accessed May 23, 2020. https://www.hrw.org/world-report/2018/country-chapters/eritrea

8. Frantzman S. Sisi, crack down on mass murder, torture in Sinai! *The Jerusalem Post | JPost.com.* https://www.jpost.com/opinion/columnists/sisi-crack-down-on-mass-murder-torture-in-sinai-360204. Published June 22, 2014. Accessed June 8, 2020.

9. Greenwood P. Sinai desert plagued by kidnap and torture – as the authorities bury their heads. *The Guardian.* https://www.theguardian.com/world/2012/feb/14/egypt-bedouin-kidnap-refugees-israel. Published February 14, 2012. Accessed May 23, 2020.

10. Gittleson B. Inside Sinai's Torture Camps. *The Atlantic.* Published November 14, 2012. Accessed May 23, 2020. https://www.theatlantic.com/international/archive/2012/11/inside-sinais-torture-camps/265204/

11. Goor Y. *Ransom Kidnapping and Human Trafficking: The Case of the Sinai Torture Camps.* Social Science Research Network; 2017. Accessed May 23, 2020. https://papers.ssrn.com/abstract=3019436

12. Simpson G. *"I Wanted to Lie down and Die": Trafficking and Torture of Eritreans in Sudan and Egypt.* Human Rights Watch; 2014.

13. Lynch S. Sinai Becomes Prison for African Migrants. *The New York Times.* https://www.nytimes.com/2012/11/01/world/middleeast/01iht-m01-sinai-migrants.html. Published October 31, 2012. Accessed May 23, 2020.

14. Tsurkov E. The New Torture Camps for Eritrean Asylum-Seekers. Hotline. Published June 10, 2015. Accessed May 23, 2020. https://hotline.org.il/en/the-new-torture-camps-for-eritrean-asylum-seekers/

15. Goldman P, Bruton FB. Israel's plan to deport thousands of migrants prompts soul-searching. NBC News. Published February 7, 2018. Accessed May 23, 2020. https://www.nbcnews.com/news/mideast/israel-s-plan-deport-african-migrants-prompts-soul-searching-n845021

Chapter Ten: The Happiness of Pursuit

1. Sanderson B. *The Way of Kings.* First edition. Tor Fantasy; 2011.

2. Bailey NW, Freedman G, Raj K, et al. Mindfulness meditators show altered distributions of early and late neural activity markers of attention in a response inhibition task. *PLoS One.* 2019;14(8). doi:10.1371/journal.pone.0203096

3. Trotter RJ. Stress: Confusion & Controversy. *Science News.* 1975;107(22):356-359. doi:10.2307/3959836

4. Jamieson J, Mendes W, Blackstock E, Schmader T. Turning the knots in your stomach into bows: Reappraising arousal improves performance on the GRE. *Journal of experimental social psychology.* 2010;46:208-212. doi:10.1016/j.jesp.2009.08.015

5. Saad MJ, Morais SL, Saad ST. Reduced cortisol secretion in patients with iron deficiency. *Ann Nutr Metab.* 1991;35(2):111-115. doi:10.1159/000177633

6. The Royal College of Pathologists of Australasia. *Position Statement: The Use of Iron Studies, Ferritin and Other Tests of Iron Status.*; 2017. Accessed

May 23, 2020. https://www.rcpa.edu.au/Library/College-Policies/
Position-Statements/The-Use-of-Iron-Studies,-Ferritin-and-Other-
Tests

7. Schutte NS, Malouff JM, Keng S-L. Meditation and telomere length: a
meta-analysis. *Psychol Health*. Published online January 5, 2020:1-15. doi
:10.1080/08870446.2019.1707827

8. Epel ES, Blackburn EH, Lin J, et al. Accelerated telomere shortening
in response to life stress. *Proc Natl Acad Sci U S A*. 2004;101(49):17312-
17315. doi:10.1073/pnas.0407162101

9. Epel E, Daubenmier J, Moskowitz JT, Folkman S, Blackburn E. Can
meditation slow rate of cellular aging? Cognitive stress, mindfulness,
and telomeres. *Ann N Y Acad Sci*. 2009;1172:34-53. doi:10.1111/j.1749-
6632.2009.04414.x

10. Schutte NS, Malouff JM, Keng S-L. *Op cit.*

11. Mendioroz M, Puebla-Guedea M, Montero-Marín J, et al. Telomere
length correlates with subtelomeric DNA methylation in long-term
mindfulness practitioners. *Sci Rep*. 2020;10. doi:10.1038/s41598-020-
61241-6

12. National Institute of Environmental Health Sciences. Environmental
Epigenetics. National Institute of Environmental Health Sciences.
Published 2020. Accessed May 23, 2020. https://www.niehs.nih.gov/
research/supported/health/envepi/index.cfm

13. Olden K, Lin Y-S, Gruber D, Sonawane B. Epigenome: Biosensor of
Cumulative Exposure to Chemical and Nonchemical Stressors Related
to Environmental Justice. *Am J Public Health*. 2014;104(10):1816-1821.
doi:10.2105/AJPH.2014.302130

14. Bell JT, Spector TD. A twin approach to unraveling epigenetics. *Trends
Genet*. 2011;27(3):116-125. doi:10.1016/j.tig.2010.12.005

15. Kaliman P, Alvarez-López MJ, Cosín-Tomás M, Rosenkranz
MA, Lutz A, Davidson RJ. Rapid changes in histone
deacetylases and inflammatory gene expression in expert
meditators. *Psychoneuroendocrinology*. 2014;40:96-107. doi:10.1016/j.
psyneuen.2013.11.004

16. Weaver ICG, Cervoni N, Champagne FA, et al. Epigenetic programming by maternal behavior. *Nature Neuroscience.* 2004;7(8):847-854. doi:10.1038/nn1276

17. Cummins RA. On the trail of the gold standard for subjective well-being. *Soc Indic Res.* 1995;35(2):179-200. doi:10.1007/BF01079026

18. Diener E, Lucas RE, Scollon CN. Beyond the hedonic treadmill: revising the adaptation theory of well-being. *Am Psychol.* 2006;61(4):305-314. doi:10.1037/0003-066X.61.4.305

19. Brickman P, Coates D, Janoff-Bulman R. Lottery winners and accident victims: is happiness relative? *J Pers Soc Psychol.* 1978;36(8):917-927. doi:10.1037//0022-3514.36.8.917

20. Bartels M, Boomsma DI. Born to be Happy? The Etiology of Subjective Well-Being. *Behav Genet.* 2009;39(6):605. doi:10.1007/s10519-009-9294-8

21. Lykken D, Tellegen A. Happiness Is a Stochastic Phenomenon: *Psychological Science.* Published online May 6, 2016. Accessed May 23, 2020. https://journals.sagepub.com/doi/10.1111/j.1467-9280.1996.tb00355.x

22. Røysamb E, Harris JR, Magnus P, Vittersø J, Tambs K. Subjective well-being. Sex-specific effects of genetic and environmental factors. *Personality and Individual Differences.* 2002;32(2):211-223. doi:10.1016/S0191-8869(01)00019-8

23. Stubbe JH, Posthuma D, Boomsma DI, Geus EJCD. Heritability of life satisfaction in adults: a twin-family study. *Psychological Medicine.* 2005;35(11):1581-1588. doi:10.1017/S0033291705005374

24. Nes RB, Røysamb E, Tambs K, Harris JR, Reichborn-Kjennerud T. Subjective well-being: genetic and environmental contributions to stability and change. *Psychological Medicine.* 2006;36(7):1033-1042. doi:10.1017/S0033291706007409

25. Lykken D, Tellegen A. *Op cit.*

26. Cummins RA. Understanding Quality of Life in Medicine: A New Approach. *J Am Coll Nutr.* 2015;34 Suppl 1:4-9. doi:10.1080/07315724.2015.1080099

27. Cruz AV de la. "But what is happiness? It's the moment before you need more happiness." My Geek Wisdom. Published September 8, 2018. Accessed June 9, 2020. https://mygeekwisdom.com/2018/09/08/but-what-is-happiness-its-the-moment-before-you-need-more-happiness/

28. Staddon JER, Cerutti DT. Operant Conditioning. *Annu Rev Psychol.* 2003;54:115-144. doi:10.1146/annurev.psych.54.101601.145124

29. Wright R. *Why Buddhism Is True: The Science and Philosophy of Meditation and Enlightenment.* Simon & Schuster; 2017.

30. Bodhi B. *The Noble Eightfold Path.* Access to Insight; 1998. http://www.buddhanet.net/pdf_file/noble8path6.pdf

31. Desbordes G, Gard T, Hoge EA, et al. Moving beyond Mindfulness: Defining Equanimity as an Outcome Measure in Meditation and Contemplative Research. *Mindfulness (N Y).* 2015;6(2):356-372. doi:10.1007/s12671-013-0269-8

32. Cummins RA. Subjective Wellbeing, Homeostatically Protected Mood and Depression: A Synthesis. *J Happiness Stud.* 2010;11(1):1-17. doi:10.1007/s10902-009-9167-0

Epilogue: My Life of Living Mindfully

1. Antonakakis N, Collins A. The impact of fiscal austerity on suicide mortality: Evidence across the 'Eurozone periphery.' *Social Science & Medicine.* 2015;145:63-78. doi:10.1016/j.socscimed.2015.09.033

2. Brooks SK, Webster RK, Smith LE, et al. The psychological impact of quarantine and how to reduce it: rapid review of the evidence. *The Lancet.* 2020;395(10227):912-920. doi:10.1016/S0140-6736(20)30460-8

3. Sullivan D, von Wachter T. Job Displacement and Mortality: An Analysis Using Administrative Data. *Q J Econ.* 2009;124(3):1265-1306. doi:10.1162/qjec.2009.124.3.1265

4. Bonanno G, Galea S, Bucciarelli A, Vlahov D. Psychological Resilience After Disaster: New York City in the Aftermath of the September 11th Terrorist Attack. *Psychological Science.* 2006;17:181-186. doi:10.1111/j.1467-9280.2006.01682.x

5. Patel V, Saxena S, Lund C, et al. The Lancet Commission on global mental health and sustainable development. *The Lancet.* 2018;392(10157):1553-1598. doi:10.1016/S0140-6736(18)31612-X

6. World Health Organisation. Depression. Published 2020. Accessed May 21, 2020. https://www.who.int/news-room/fact-sheets/detail/depression

7. MacKenzie MB, Abbott KA, Kocovski NL. Mindfulness-based cognitive therapy in patients with depression: current perspectives. *Neuropsychiatr Dis Treat.* 2018;14:1599-1605. doi:10.2147/NDT.S160761

8. Tapper K. Mindfulness and craving: effects and mechanisms. *Clin Psychol Rev.* 2018;59:101-117. doi:10.1016/j.cpr.2017.11.003

9. Hilton L, Hempel S, Ewing BA, et al. Mindfulness Meditation for Chronic Pain: Systematic Review and Meta-analysis. *Ann Behav Med.* 2017;51(2):199-213. doi:10.1007/s12160-016-9844-2

10. Semple RJ, Droutman V, Reid BA. Mindfulness Goes To School: Things Learned (So Far) From Research and Real-world Experiences. *Psychol Sch.* 2017;54(1):29-52. doi:10.1002/pits.21981

11. Guendelman S, Medeiros S, Rampes H. Mindfulness and emotion regulation: Insights from neurobiological, psychological, and clinical studies. *Frontiers in Psychology.* 2017;8(MAR). doi:10.3389/fpsyg.2017.00220

12. World Health Organisation. Mental health: massive scale-up of resources needed if global targets are to be met. WHO. Published June 6, 2018. Accessed May 23, 2020. http://www.who.int/mental_health/evidence/atlas/atlas_2017_web_note/en/

AGAINST BEING AGAINST
ACKNOWLEDGEMENTS

As is my way, I did a little research before sitting down to write my acknowledgements and came across a 2012 opinion piece published in the *New Yorker* titled 'Against Acknowledgements', in which book reviewer Sam Sacks writes a 1500-word essay vehemently arguing against the long-running tradition. His point is that when there's champagne to sip and cake to eat, no one really wants to hear the bride and groom wax lyrical about their wonderful friends and family.

Sacks argues that, because writing is such a solitary endeavour, on the 'off chance' that the intended recipients of acknowledgements really *did* help in a meaningful way with the creation of the book, including them on a list that 'looks like the bcc line of a mass email' is pretty poor form.

He's right, of course. Gratitude in 12pt font is woefully inadequate for expressing my sincere thanks to the people who made this book and the *My Year of Living Mindfully* project possible. But I do nevertheless feel it needs to be immortalised in print. There's a good reason the greeting card industry is worth around $7.5 *billion*: as people, we rather like to say heartfelt thank yous.

So at the risk of droning on like an overinflated actor at the Oscars, I'd like to express my gratitude to:

The dedicated and talented team who worked on the *My Year of Living Mindfully* documentary, including the gifted cinematographers Dan Martland and Chris Bland, graphics whiz Luke Harris, music dynamos Dave Chapman and Derek Allan, post-coordinator and impact producer Hattie O'Connor, and publicist Jackie Evans. I know I pulled one too many favours but I hope you'll all still take my call next time.

The team at Hachette – publisher Sophie Hamley, project editor Stacey Clair, copyeditor Rod Morrison and proofreader Alex Craig. Sophie, thank you for seeing this was a 'thing' before it was even close to looking like one. And to the whole team for smoothing over my incorrectly speled names, gramtical faux pahs, superfluous turns of fraze, unnecessary elaboration (when I needlessly over explained and delineated without adding anything interesting, useful or entertaining in order to slowly and painfully progress the evolving story along) and also for your kind and gentle nudges to do better. With a Master's in journalism, you would have thought that I would know that meditation 'practice' and sitting down to 'practise' meditation are two different words by now, but no.

Quinn Denel, Joyce Meko and the team at Tugboat Studios for the imaginative illustrations. Your pictures eloquently say more than my thousands of words.

The scientists, researchers and experts who donated their time, energy and knowledge for interviews and advice. I finally understand what you meant when you explained that no matter how far we might probe, we will only ever encounter further mysteries. Especially to Craig Hassed, Amit Bernstein, Willem Kuyken and Judson Brewer, and to the Australian team of scientists who signed on to track me for a year; Neil Bailey, Jonathan Davies, Hilda Pickett, Marc Wilkins, Nicolas Cherbuin, Kimina Lyall, Marc Longster, and my doctor, Anna Finniss. A special thanks to Jonno, who magnanimously helped with the references and last-minute additions for the book.

To Linda and Tony Bloom and Sharon Deutsch-Nadir from The Bloom Foundation. It is such a relief knowing there are people like you in the world and that you believe in the importance of evidence-backed information as much as I do.

To Molly Harries, whose own dreams went belly-up when COVID-19 struck but who unflinchingly made it possible for us to still release ours into the world.

To my best friend, Liz Neil, for your constant encouragement, fearless conversation and kind-hearted provocation. And to my sister, Justine Taylor, who is *always* there. No matter what.

To my mother, Kerry Jones, who leads by example with courage, strength, generosity and compassion. You taught me to set a destination and how to stay the course even in the dead of night with a broken compass.

To my mother- and father-in-law, Max and Alice Harvey. For 'launch-pie', wise counsel, unwavering support, home maintenance, free babysitting and unreserved love. I've known you for exactly half my lifetime now and your influence is immeasurable.

To my children. Thank you for waiting while I wrote this. Yes, now we can play UNO.

And finally and most importantly to my husband, Julian (Jules) Harvey, the co-director, writer, cinematographer, editor, executive producer, digital producer, web designer, brand advisor, child wrangler, 24-hour counsellor, dish washer, house cleaner, wardrobe consultant, caterer, gardener, head of maintenance, and cheerleader-in-chief. A man with an uncanny ability to hold things together with nothing but cardboard and Gaffa tape, and whose unquestioned belief in my ability makes me work harder so that he's not proven wrong.

To all these people, inadequate though it may be, I'd like to say thank you. Along with a copy of this book, you will find more than just words. Please find attached tickets for an all-expenses paid, one-month holiday on a private island on the Great Barrier Reef. Just kidding. It's a bottle of organic wine.

For more information about Shannon Harvey's blogs,
podcasts, documentaries and new experiments,
visit www.shannonharvey.com